Go as Gold

The Power of a Positive Mental Attitude

The
Napoleon
Hill
Foundation
—

Napoleon Hill

with Judith Williamson

JAICO PUBLISHING HOUSE

Ahmedabad Bangalore Bhopal Bhubaneswar Chennai
Delhi Hyderabad Kolkata Lucknow Mumbai

Published by Jaico Publishing House
A-2 Jash Chambers, 7-A Sir Phirozshah Mehta Road
Fort, Mumbai - 400 001
jaicopub@jaicobooks.com
www.jaicobooks.com

© The Napoleon Hill Foundation

Published in arrangement with
The Napoleon Hill Foundation
PO Box 1277
Wise, Virginia USA 24293

To be sold only in India, Bangladesh, Bhutan,
Pakistan, Nepal, Sri Lanka and the Maldives.

GOOD AS GOLD
ISBN 978-81-8495-186-8

First Jaico Impression: 2010
Ninth Jaico Impression: 2018

Printed by
Concept Imprint Pvt. Ltd.
Plot No. 51/1/4, Site IV, Industrial Area
Sahibabad, Ghaziabad - 201010 (UP)

Photo presented to The Napoleon Hill Foundation in 2010 from the private collection of Napoleon Hill's grandson, Dr. J. B. Hill.

PREFACE

In Webster's New World Dictionary GOLD is defined as both a precious metal and money. Standard is defined as something used as a basis or rule of comparison in measuring and demonstrating reliability and/or approval. Upon reviewing the works of Dr. Napoleon Hill, it is not difficult to understand why Judith Williamson chose *Napoleon Hill: Good as Gold* as the appropriate title for this book on life's riches. Beginning his writings as a 13 year old living in the mountains of Southwest Virginia and continuing on for seven decades, Dr. Hill honed his writing ability. He mined for gold in the lives of those he researched and documented in his major works that include *Law of Success* and *Think and Grow Rich*. Over his lifetime, his readership inherited his golden legacy in the form of all his written works.

Judith Williamson is a long time advocate of Dr. Hill's success principles. She studies them, teaches the *Keys to Success Course* at Purdue University, and presents seminars, workshops, and lecturing engagements that have taken her to the far points of the globe. Her knowledge, speaking ability and presentations have been praised by participants worldwide. Additionally, Judy has Dr. Napoleon Hill's archives housed at the Napoleon Hill World Learning Center located on the campus of Purdue University-Calumet in Hammond, Indiana. Herein is a wealth of information, some personal, and some historical but of tremendous value for its content and interest for devotees of Napoleon Hill.

The material in the Napoleon Hill World Learning Center's archives includes original copies of Hill's magazines. From 1919 to 1923, Hill had two monthly magazines–*Napoleon Hill's Magazine* and *Napoleon Hill's Golden Rules Magazine*. In *A Lifetime of Riches*, Hill's biography by Michael J. Ritt, Jr. and Kirk Landers, it is stated that the magazines should not have been successful at the time, but they were. Starting on a small budget, Hill did the writing, editing and selling himself. As Hill panned for gold in the success stream of life, he began to enrich himself and others with what he uncovered.

You will be greatly rewarded if you read the articles Ms. Williamson presents in *Napoleon Hill: Good as Gold*. Some of these will appeal to your particular need due to where you are on your success journey. If you study the material and find that a trait such as flexibility is lacking in your character, you should read the article again thoroughly and make the necessary changes in your behavior so you too can mine the gold from the information.

As a former bank president, I thoroughly endorse *Napoleon Hill: Good as Gold* as a source of riches that you can take to the bank! Your profit from the book will materialize in the riches you uncover while living your life's purpose. Knowing what to do is great, but applying what you have learned is the real secret to success. You gain your greatest riches in life when you read, study, and take action on what you have learned.

Don Green, Executive Director
The Napoleon Hill Foundation

INTRODUCTION

It is my pleasure to share with you readings from Napoleon Hill's writings that range from his earliest to his latest works. Selections are included from his essays, his books, and his capstone course: *PMA Science of Success*. In addressing these writings, I enjoyed fast forwarding to today's current application of his philosophy. Remembering that "there is nothing new under the sun," it is refreshing to align Dr. Hill's thoughts with my interpretation and application of them in today's ever changing world.

Whether you are a student, a businessman, an entrepreneur, or a teacher, you will glean much information from the shared material in this volume. Dr. Hill was and still continues to be the inspiration for many self-help books, management books, and educational materials that expand on his 17 Principles of Success.

I know of no better teacher under which to begin the examination of your own life and performance. By using the shared secrets uncovered during his lifetime of research and practice, Dr. Hill guides you step by step in becoming the person you were meant to be.

This material is pure, unadulterated gold, and hence the title of the book: *Napoleon Hill: Good as Gold*.

In studying any self-help motivational material, it is always a worthy choice to trace the material back to its original source. When you go on this treasure hunt using Dr. Hill's writings you will not come up empty handed. Rather, as you prospect for gold your investment of time will pay off in increased earnings in your field of choice.

So, I commend you to the material. There are 52

chapters–that equates to one per week. Read a little, reflect a lot, and then when you uncover the secret, put it into immediate action. As Dr. Hill states:

When a plan comes through to your conscious mind while you are open to the guidance of Infinite Intelligence, accept it with appreciation and gratitude and act on it at once. Do not hesitate, do not argue, challenge, worry, fret about it, or wonder if it's right. Act on it!

By reading this book you are acting on your explicit faith that you can become the person you desire to be. By raising your sights to your "higher self" you are visualizing the picture perfect outcome for your purpose and plan here on Earth.

Enjoy your journey. Enjoy the book.

Judith Williamson

GOOD ᴬˢ GOLD
1

If we view success as not necessarily finding the pot of gold at the end of the rainbow but being able to meet the challenges we encounter as we go about trying to attain our Definite Major Purpose, we will be able to remain positive.

—Eliezer A. Alperstein, CPA

Today we are hearing more and more about the necessity for change. Change is required to avoid the accumulation of many harmful traits such as complacency, stagnation, inertia, resistance, sluggishness, and self-satisfaction. Those who are not desirous of change are said to be caught in a comfort zone most often of their own making. If allowed, comfort zones become ruts that we fall into and eventually become graves. If we allow our attitudes to become "grayish," we risk becoming old and spent before our time.

How does one embrace change? I have heard that one way is to respond to a suggestion for change with "yes, and . . ." rather than "yes, but . . . " The first response is open and offers additional ideas, while the second more common, more "polite" way tends to be veiled criticism. By saying "yes, but . . ." one is really negating the idea being put forward. This is often termed constructive criticism. On the other hand, by saying "yes, and . . ." the door remains open for acceptance and the ongoing opportunity to mingle ideas instead of verbally slamming the door in someone's face.

Our attitudes can become hardened like our arteries.

Our mental diet is as significant or perhaps more significant than our regular eating plan. It has been said that we are what we eat. Also, obviously we are what we think. Mental and physical characteristics go hand in hand. Have you ever heard someone called a sourpuss, a scatterbrain, a flake, a parasite, or even a jackass? These are not meant to be complimentary terms, however, they are representative of attitudes that have so hardened that they now take on physical characteristics. Wouldn't it be better to be known as a sweetheart, an angel, a gentleman, a leader, or even a mover and a shaker?

We can change our personality descriptors by changing our attitudes. Attitudes color our disposition and then slowly but systematically mold our character. Character then determines our destiny. Change begins inside each one of us and expands to the outer limits of our physical selves. Next, the energy we generate touches those whom we come into contact with in a contagious way. Do you wish to be the harbinger of sickness or health? Goodness or evil? Heaven or Hell? The answer lies in the attitude that you display for the world to see. If yours isn't what you envision it to be, it's time to make a change. Begin today by saying "yes" instead of "no" as opportunities present themselves. View life as a gift waiting to be unwrapped, not as a delete function on your keyboard. It will make all the difference to your future if you open yourself and embrace opportunities that come to you daily. In the end, you will be the better for it.

The Importance of Change
by Napoleon Hill

Of the utmost significance is the fact that the Creator provided man with the one and only means by which he has broken away from the animal family and ascended into spiritual estates, where he may be the master of his own earthly fate. The means thus provided is the law of change. By the simple process of changing his mental attitude, man can draw for himself any pattern of life and living he chooses and make that pattern a reality. This is the one and only thing over which man has been provided with irrevocable, unchallenged, and unchallengeable powers of absolute control–a fact which suggests that it must have been considered by the Creator to be the most important prerogative of man.

Dictators and would-be world conquerors come and they go. They always *go* because it is not a part of the overall plan of the universe for man to be enslaved. It is rather a part of the eternal pattern that every man shall be free, to live his own life his own way, to control his thoughts and his deeds, to make his own earthly destiny.

That is why the philosopher, who looks backward into the past to determine what is going to happen in the yet unborn future, cannot get excited because a Hitler or a Stalin momentarily basks in the light of his own ego and threatens the freedom of mankind. For these men, like all others of their ilk who have preceded them, will destroy themselves with their own excesses and vanities and their lusts for power over the free world. Moreover, these would-be stranglers of human freedom may be only demons who unwittingly serve as shock troops to awaken man from his complacency and make way for the change that will bring new and better ways of living.

Nature leads man through change after change by peaceful means as long as man cooperates, but she resorts to revolutionary methods if man rebels and neglects or refuses to conform to the law of change. The revolutionary method may consist of the death of a loved one or a severe illness; it may bring a failure in business, or the loss of a job, which forces the individual to change his occupation and seek employment in an entirely new field, where he will find greater opportunities which he would never have known if his old habits had not been broken up.

Nature enforces the law of fixation of habits in every living thing lower than man, and just as definitely enforces the law of change in the habits of man. Nature thus provides the only means by which man may grow and evolve in accordance with his fixed position in the overall plan of the universe.

Thomas A. Edison's first major adversity was experienced when his teacher sent him home after only three months in a grade school, with a note to his parents saying he did not have the capacity to take an education. He never went back to school–a conventional school, that is–but he began to school himself in the great University of Hard Knocks, where he gained an education which made him one of the greatest inventors of all times. Before he was graduated from that university he was fired from one job after another, while the hand of Destiny guided him through the *essential changes* which prepared him to become a great inventor. A formal schooling perhaps would have spoiled his chances of becoming great.

Nature knows what she is about when adversity, physical pain, sorrow, distress, failure and temporary defeat overtake one. Remember this and profit by it the next time you meet with adversity. And instead of crying out in rebellion, or shivering with fear, hold your head high and look in all directions for that seed of an equivalent benefit which is carried in every circumstance of adversity.

Source: *You Can Work Your Own Miracles*. Napoleon Hill.
Fawcett Columbine, New York. Pgs. 33 & 34.

GOOD AS GOLD
2

As you know, the seed of all success is Definiteness of Purpose. Often we talk about using a road map: without a specific destination, you can't choose a route.

–Christopher Lake

Here are five facts worth remembering:
1) Thoughts are things.
2) Our choices create our outcomes in life.
3) What we think about we become.
4) A positive mental attitude is the right mental attitude in all circumstances.
5) Our mind can only entertain one thought and/or emotion at a time.

These simple, yet powerful statements can change your life. By putting these ideas into positive daily action, a "ho-hum" mundane existence can blossom into something miraculous. Just as the butterfly transitions from the earthbound caterpillar and takes to the air, so too can this magical metamorphosis occur in your life. The pattern of existence seems to indicate that first one grows roots and then wings. As your wings begin to bud, expand, and prepare you for flight, why not work to better understand the aerodynamics of your invisible self?

Two fantastic books that do just this are: *Your Greatest Power* and *How to Become a Mental Millionaire.* Don Green, the Executive Director of the Napoleon Hill

Foundation, states that: "Many people can't be successful in the best of times because they have failed to make use of THIS GREATEST POWER . . . THE POWER TO CHOOSE. Other people will apply THIS GREATEST POWER . . . THE POWER TO CHOOSE . . .and be successful even in bad times because they refuse to let adversity stop them . . . they will persist until they succeed."

These times can be viewed optimistically or pessimistically depending upon the mindset one creates. Good always exists within the bad, and vice versa. Training yourself to focus on the good enables you to recognize the good when it presents itself in your life. Likewise focusing on the bad, attracts more of the same to you because you have set up an antenna for it. Thoughts migrate just like birds and fish. There is an instinctual homing device that directs their movements. Unlike creatures that are programmed by instinct, man creates his own patterns. What patterns are you designing for your life? You DO have the power to choose. Choose wisely and on purpose.

Your Unused Riches
by Napoleon Hill

"Do the thing," said Emerson,
"and you shall have the power."

Your greatest asset is one which you may not have properly evaluated.

It is the one asset with which you may lift yourself into whatever position or circumstance you desire, and it is one you can never lose through the perfidy of others, nor can it be taken from you or stolen.

It is appropriately called your "greatest asset" because it is the one thing over which you have complete, unchallengeable power of control, and it must have been so regarded by your Creator because it is the only thing over which you were given the exclusive usage.

14

Your greatest asset is your privilege of taking possession of your own mind and directing it to the attainment of purposes of your own choice.

This exclusive privilege carries with it profound riches as a reward for your using it wisely, and unmerciful penalties for your failure to embrace and use it wisely.

Among the riches with which you will be regarded for controlling and directing your own mind are financial security–sound health–peace of mind–the affection of friends and loved ones–and a station in life of your own choice.

Among the penalties you may have to pay for failure to take possession of your own mind are poverty–ill health–fear and worry–loss of friends–and *unanswered prayers*.

Your mind was given to you to be used for all your needs in the business of negotiating your way through life in a style of your own choice. Like any organ or muscle of your body, the brain in which your mind functions will atrophy and wither away through disuse.

The highest and the noblest use you can make of your mind is by development of a sixth sense through which you may communicate with the source of all wisdom when you pray.

And the more you depend upon prayer for guidance in all of your acts, the stronger will your mindpower become, until there will come a time when you may communicate with Infinite Intelligence instantaneously at will.

The late Charles P. Steinmetz once expressed the belief that the time would come when the act of prayer would be as scientific and as definite as the rules of mathematics or the laws of physics. Other great thinkers have expressed a similar belief.

Source: *Success Unlimited*.

Your greatest asset is your privilege of taking possession of a strong mind, a [illegible] and [illegible] of your own career?

This exclusive privilege [illegible] with [illegible] is your reward for [illegible] and [illegible] benefits [illegible] you allowed to embrace and use it wisely.

Through the [illegible] which man will be [illegible] in building [illegible] financial security, sound health, peace [illegible] and the [illegible] of friends and love [illegible] life [illegible] for failure [illegible]

and [illegible] measured [illegible]

This [illegible] given [illegible] to be used [illegible] through life in [illegible] of your own [illegible] in your [illegible] and [illegible] through [illegible]

[illegible]

[illegible] the [illegible] you [illegible] and [illegible] guidance [illegible] all [illegible] the strong will [illegible] and the [illegible] will.

The late [illegible] the [illegible] world [illegible] of the [illegible] Other [illegible] have expressed a similar belief.

GOOD ^{AS} GOLD
3

Napoleon Hill describes it best. A pleasing personality is the sum total of your mental, spiritual, and physical traits which distinguish you from all others.

–Loretta Levin

Developing a pleasing personality is one of the most important rungs on the ladder to success. Time invested in the acquisition of this trait will pay high dividends now and in your future. Consider for a moment those individuals whom you know that possess a genuine, pleasing personality. I am not referring to salesmen who could convince you to buy a mint TRS 80 Computer that belongs in the Smithsonian, but rather the person who lights up a room, holds a two-way conversation with you and leaves you feeling the better for it, generates enthusiasm where none was before, and has a charisma that goes beyond words. Get a visual image of that person in your mind's eye, and next determine that you will mirror those very traits in yourself to become just like the person you decide to model.

Now, the next step is to put your plan into action. Ask yourself what improvements your personality could use, and then decide to cultivate those traits one at a time. For example, do you talk more than you listen? Do you cut people off before they finish their sentence? Do you negate their ideas in favor of your own for no valid reason? Do you diminish their importance by not focusing on them when they are in your presence? Do you neglect to say "please" and "thank you" when interacting with them? Are you forever asking for assistance but offering none in return? All of the above noted things can cause you to have a less than pleasing personality in the eyes of others. And, like it or not, it's not your impression of who you are, but the impressions others report that count in your overall evaluation.

Two little things that you can do right this minute to improve your personality score are to smile and to listen. When you greet others with a smile on your face, you encourage them to give you one in return. This exchange of smiles raises the positive atmosphere and allows good thoughts to begin flowing between the two of you. Also, by listening first and speaking second, you might just become a person people like to talk to and, more importantly, by truly listening to others you may learn something in the process. Neither one of these actions is difficult, but they can and do make a huge difference in others' perceptions of you.

So, just for today, give it a try. Tonight, if you think back and determine that it made a positive difference in your outcome by smiling and listening, decide to add these two actions to your success toolkit. Soon you will begin the interior decorating that will transform your physical home into a very hospitable environment.

How to Develop a Pleasing Personality
by Napoleon Hill

"Your personality is the sample case in which you display what you have to offer."

The thing which heads the entire list of causes of failure is *inability to get along pleasantly with people*. It has been said that the late Franklin D. Roosevelt's pleasing personality made him the most successful politician we have ever known.

Charles M. Schwab's pleasing personality lifted him from manual labor to a $75,000.00 per year position, and in addition to this he often received a bonus of ten times that amount.

You can have a "million dollar personality" if you will follow these instructions:

- Develop a positive mental attitude and express it in all of your relations with others.

- Train your voice by always speaking in a pleasing tone that will denote friendliness.

- Follow the habit of alertness of mind and a willingness to listen with interest when others are conversing with you. "Getting someone else told" may feed the ego but it never attracts friends.

- Make yourself flexible in all your relations with others by adjusting yourself to all circumstances without losing your composure, and remember that the "other fellow's" silence may be greater than your words when you are angry.

- Develop the habit of patience, and remember that proper timing in all of your words and deeds may give you a big advantage over the impatient person's.

- Keep an open mind on all subjects, toward all people, for it is an established fact that favorable opportunities never break down the doors to closed minds, and intolerance does not lead to wisdom.

- Learn to smile when you are speaking to others and thereby disarm them of any feeling that you are not a friendly person.

- Be tactful in your speech and manner, keeping in mind that not all thoughts should be expressed even if they are accurate.

- Follow the habit of promptness in decisions and remember that procrastination *reveals to others a negative trait of personality.*

- Engage in at least one good deed each day in which you will praise or serve one or more people without expectation of reward, and observe how rapidly your list of friends will grow.

These ten steps to a pleasing personality are yours for the taking.

Source: *Success Unlimited*.

GOOD ᴬˢ GOLD
4

Tolerance is an internal governor urging us to not jump to conclusions about a person or idea so we won't miss the benefit, the beauty, and the learning.
—Mary Foley

Napoleon Hill's advice is as pertinent today as when it was written decades ago. His views on Tolerance should be memorized by anyone who is interested in being an agent of change in the world. With change comes growth. With change comes renewal. With change comes spring and rebirth. Tolerance oftentimes precedes change and prepares the individual for new learning experiences. If viewed as a catalyst, it leads a person to new opportunities for advancement in today's world. It may be likened to evolution of the spirit where small daily changes converge to create a monumental change of insight. Without being willing to suspend disbelief, that is, without being tolerant of something new, no critical change can occur.

Being tolerant requires that personal beliefs, values, interests, attitudes, and ideas are held in abeyance for a time. This temporary suspension of what one knows to be "true" enables new ideas to present themselves for consideration. Much like shopping for new clothing, the trying on experience helps a person determine whether to buy or not. When new ideas are tried on for a cognitive fit, the person determines whether or not the idea can be incorporated into his mental wardrobe. If the answer is "yes," the personal choices grow, if the answer is "no," then the choices are the same ones that have been made before.

Change is the heartbeat of the Universe. It is alive and growing. It propels us forward. It creates motion and movement. Tolerance opens the door and invites us to welcome change. It is a handshake that can lead to brotherhood. It is an inclusive circle that draws one inside, rather than being exclusionary. It unites rather than divides.

So, when faced with an opportunity to be spontaneous and open, accept it. Explore the opportunity for a fit. If it works for you, use it. If not, know that you have tried and because you have tried you are the better for it. However, if the shoe doesn't fit, you're not obliged to wear it. You can always practice first to make perfect later. As Emerson states: "Do the thing and you shall have the power." It was good advice then and it is good advice now.

Tolerance–A Philosopher's Creed
by Napoleon Hill

Let me be open-minded on all subjects so that I may grow mentally and spiritually.

May the time never come when I will be above learning from the humblest person.

Let me never forget that a closed mind is a narrow mind.

May I never fall into the bad habit of expressing opinions on any subject unless they are founded upon reasonably dependable knowledge.

Forbid that I should ever find fault with anyone because he may not agree with my opinions on any subject.

Restrain me always, Oh Power of Reason, from speaking out of turn, where I have not been invited to speak.

May I always show a wholesome respect for those with whom I may not agree.

Keep me ever reminded that the thing I know best is that I know too little about anything; that the sum total of knowledge acquired by the whole of mankind is not enough to justify any man in boasting of his knowledge.

Give me the courage to admit that I do not know when I am asked a question about which I know but little or nothing.

May I always share willingly such humble knowledge as I may possess which could be of help to others.

And never let me forget that humility of the heart will attract more friends than will all the wisdom of mankind.

Let me remain always a student, in search of truth, and may I never pretend to be a finished scholar on any subject.

And may I always remember that the greatest of all privileges is that of expressing tolerance by example.

Give me some good books, some loyal friends with whom I dare to be myself, and never let me forget the words, "Hope, Faith, and Charity."

Source: *Success Unlimited*. August 1955. Vol II, No. VII, Pg. 25.

GOOD ^{AS} GOLD
5

Reading–more than any other activity–has the power to unlock our potential and, in the process, unleash the "better angels of our nature," to quote Abraham Lincoln, a man who raised himself from a country boy to President of the United States by reading books, establishing a goal, and relentlessly and persistently working toward that goal.

—Gail Brooks

If you do nothing else but read to a child, you are providing a great service. It's been said that "Readers are Leaders," and in order to grow a leader you must engender in youth a love for reading. By my own admission, I am a "book-a-holic." And, I will tell you a little secret. Don Green, the Executive Director for the Foundation is too. We both simply love books and reading. Don brags that he has several books on his nightstand that he reads simultaneously. My husband states that I have a good portion of the Library of Congress in our home. I favor self-help literature because of the work that I do, but my overall interest in books is varied. I believe that my mother brought my awareness to reading and what books could do for a person well before I could read by myself.

In an email that I recently received from Dr. J. B. Hill, Napoleon Hill's grandson, he enlightened me regarding some educational issues he uncovered while doing genealogy work on the Hill family. Dr. J. B. Hill states:

Women have always been the source of essential

education in the Hill family. My Irish mother taught me to read; my grandmother taught my dad to read before he was 5, my step great grandmother civilized and educated Napoleon, and my GG grandmother probably educated Napoleon's father. Last week, I watched my bride Nancy teaching our daughter to read and realized that it will be the same in this generation. I have the role of protector, provider, disciplinarian, ethics instructor, and Daddy—but Nancy is the real teacher to my children.

In response, I replied:

Sounds like you have really traced the Hill family history and uncovered trends that will benefit future generations. My mother too taught me to read. I was lazy in first grade because my mother read to me so much and I enjoyed it. It was a favorite pastime of mine. However, when the first grade teacher threatened to hold me back because I couldn't read, my mother countered with saying: "What do you mean, she can't read? We read all the time!" When I got home after that memorable parent-teacher conference, my mother chastised me for not reading and intuitively knew what to do. She said, "From now on, I will read to you from your favorite storybooks, but only every other page. You must read a page after I read a page."

That's all it took to get me to be an active reader not a passive listener. Mom—whose birthday is Feb. 20—has been gone since 1990, but she is in my heart every day. She was smarter than all the teachers with the degrees and teaching experience. Like the women in the Hill family, my mother knew the secret to turning on the light of learning. And, it has made all the difference to each of us, right? Today, from a first grader who couldn't/ wouldn't read, I hold a K-12 administrative license as a reading specialist among other degrees. Also, I know that the best teacher is the one nearest the pupil, not the one standing over the reluctant student trying to force-feed education. Whether it's through a typewriter or a storybook, a smart teacher knows how to catch a child's desire to learn and put it into productive action. I wish families would recognize this, and use the magic inside their children to unleash their potential. Sounds like your wife is doing a great job with your two! Congratulations.

By sharing these two personal stories with you, I hope that you begin to understand the significance of reading in a person's life. Good books lead to good thoughts that create good lives. Don't waste the opportunity to be a reader. Where else can you have a one-on-one lesson with an expert? It is the best value on the planet. Pick up a book and read! I guarantee that you will learn a great deal. Moms cannot be wrong. And, Dr. J. B. Hill, Don Green and I give reading our strongest endorsement.

Stop Making Failures of Your Children
by Napoleon Hill

Do you realize that your child's success or failure depends on you? The schooling and the religious training your children receive will play an important part in their lives, of course, but the influence they will pick up from living close to you can be and should be one that puts them on the success beam.

There are three important principles you can teach your children which will go a long way toward bringing them success and happiness throughout their lives. The first of these is Definiteness of Purpose. This habit should start when the child is very young so that it will become a fixed part of his character.

Not too long ago I was visiting friends whose little boy was playing with tinker toys. He was trying to build a helter-skelter design that soon crumbled to the floor. He began to cry when his understanding mother came to his rescue and asked him what he wanted to build.

"I dunno," he sobbed, "just something that will stand up."

"Before you start building," his mother counseled, "you must know what you want, and you must have a plan to go by. Now, let's see what you'd like to make."

After the mother had mentioned several things that could be made from the tinker toys, the youngster decided upon a small house and set to work with great enthusiasm to build it.

"This will take more time and work," cautioned the boy's father. "but when you are finished it will stand up, and you will be very proud of what you have done."

As I was getting ready to leave, the boy jubilantly grabbed me by the hand and asked me to come and look at his house "that wouldn't fall down."

"This is so much better than putting something together every which way," he exclaimed triumphantly.

On my way out to my car, the boy's father accompanied me. He was an executive in a large national chain store organization, who began as a stock clerk in one of the smaller stores, less than ten years previously. He advanced himself to a vice-presidency by following the habit of definiteness of purpose. "You understand now," he exclaimed with pride, "why we are leaving no stone unturned in seeing that our boy grows up with a full appreciation of the value of knowing what he wants."

All though your child's "when I grow up" years of wanting to be a railroad engineer, a space cadet, or a movie star, inspire in him the faith that he can be a success in whatever he chooses, but tactfully influence him to make a definite decision to work toward some specific definite major purpose in life.

The second success principle you should teach your children is the Habit of Going the Extra Mile–the rendering of useful service beyond the scope of duty. This is a "must" habit without which no one has ever been known to rise to great heights of success in any undertaking. In addition to creating favorable opportunities financially for those who follow this principle, it adds great strength to character and gives one the ability to make friends easily.

Joe and Pete were next-door neighbor sons of unskilled laborers. Neither of their parents was well schooled, but Joe's folks were wise enough to recognize the value of the habit of Going the Extra Mile, and they taught this to him from early childhood.

Pete's parents, on the other hand, impressed on him the idea of taking everything he could get without lifting a finger, and he lost no time in making this idea his own.

While his son was growing up, Joe's father was able to promote himself to a position as foreman, then department manager at his plant by following the habit of rendering more service and better service than he was actually paid for. He instilled this habit in his son.

Throughout grade school and high school Joe was a giving person–sharing generously his time in extra-curricular activities and his possessions. He was constantly going out of his way to make himself liked by both his teachers and his schoolmates. Moreover, his habit of thus Going the Extra Mile gave him great pleasure for he did it in a most pleasing mental attitude.

Meanwhile Pete did as little work as he possibly could to get by. Results, poor grades in school, difficulties with the teachers and his schoolmates, and no participation in athletics because, as he remarked, "There's no pay in it." Where did he learn this attitude? From his father who constantly griped about "slave drivers" down at the plant, in the school system, and about everywhere else.

Joe got a scholarship which paid his way through a fine college because of the excellent record he made in high school, and he went on to win high honors in college by continuing to follow the habit of Going the Extra Mile. He never asked, "What do I get out of this?" but, "What can I contribute to help someone out?"

Pete scornfully referred to Joe as "that eager beaver who tries to kill himself doing something for somebody." But the "eager beaver" did all right for himself. As the result of his college record, he wound up with the offer of a job with a wonderful company right after graduation. He still has the habit of Going the Extra Mile. It has brought him two promotions with increased pay over a number of other young men who began work with the same company when he started. The other young men had as much education as Joe, and they had as much intelligence.

What about Pete? He got a menial job right after he left high school. He moans constantly about Joe's getting all the breaks. To this day he doesn't see that Joe promoted himself into the better things of life by GIVING before trying to GET and thereby starting the great law of increasing returns to move in his favor. And Pete's parents haven't the slightest idea that they failed in preparing him for success in life.

The third success principle you should teach your child is the habit of a positive mental attitude. The habit of thinking in terms of things he can do and not in terms of things he cannot do. Henry Ford once said that what he needed most in his business organization were more men who didn't know anything about the words "it cannot be done."

Two teenage girl friends decided to try out for the freshman class play together.

When Nancy told her parents about it, they were very enthusiastic and encouraged her to go right ahead with it.

However, when Joanne told her folks, all she got was negative comments–"Why do you want to waste your time with that? Besides, your voice is too squeaky. And you'll spend too much time and catch cold in that chilly auditorium. You'll never learn all those lines, then you'll make a mistake and be embarrassed forever."

The poor girl had failed even before she started. Failed because her own parents had sold her a negative "no-can-do" mental attitude.

Nancy tried out for the play. She didn't get a part, but her positive-minded parents immediately helped her find the seed of an equivalent benefit in her temporary defeat. "Why, this will allow you to spend more time on your sewing for your 4H contest," soothed her mother. Nancy went on to win second place in the 4H contest, and she grew up to be a poised, serene wife and mother who now has two beautiful children of her own to whom she is teaching the habit of a positive mental attitude.

Joanne didn't get a part in the play either–but she didn't even try. Once she did take courage enough to overcome her parents' wails of doom and try out for the swimming team. When she didn't make the team all she got from her parents was "I told you so." Joanne today is a self-centered, withdrawn woman who spends her time and money trying all sorts of medicines to relieve her "aches and pains." Her negative mental attitude has made of her a confirmed hypochondriac.

If parents think and talk in terms of sickness and poverty and failure, they will pass these states of mind on to their children who, in turn will use them as stumbling blocks to failure throughout life. Think, act and speak in terms of health, affluence, achievement–and give your children steppingstones to success.

Source: *Success Unlimited*. November 1956, Vol. III, No. XI. Pgs. 36 & 40.

GOOD ^{AS} GOLD
6

Having faith is a tall order. Applying that faith to your life is an even taller order. But there are role models out there who can show you how it's done.

–Libby Gill

Faith is spiritual courage in an unseen positive outcome. It is knowing that what you believe in will happen with certainty. It is having an assurance that you are on the right path, and that the path–though sometimes winding–will lead you to your destiny. Faith is believing in a higher power and recognizing that this power is greater than the individual "you." However, this power still cares enough to hold you in the palm of His hand. And, most importantly, faith is the awareness that without action on your part it will be insufficient. The quotation cited by Dr. Hill states: "Faith without works is dead." This truly sums up the significance of action.

Applied faith is the catalyst that starts the wheels of success turning. It is the grease that eases movement and action. It is the yeast added to the other ingredients that causes the bread to rise. It allows you to work in a dignified and worthy manner toward your area of competency. It causes you to keep on keeping on even when the going is tough. It may not put the proverbial spring in your step, but at least it gets you out the door.

For an opposite view, I like the way Edgar Guest puts across the idea in his poem "The World is Against Me." Please reflect on what the lack of faithfulness causes to happen in a person's drive for success as you read this poem.

THE WORLD IS AGAINST ME

"The world is against me," he said with a sigh.
"Somebody stops every scheme that I try.
The world has me down and it's keeping me there;
I don't get a chance. Oh, the world is unfair!
When a fellow is poor then he can't get a show;
The world is determined to keep him down low."

"What of Abe Lincoln?" I asked. "Would you say
That he was much richer than you are today?
He hadn't your chance of making his mark,
And his outlook was often exceedingly dark;
Yet he clung to his purpose with courage most grim
And he got to the top. Was the world against him?

"What of Ben Franklin? I've oft heard it said
That many a time he went hungry to bed.
He started with nothing but courage to climb,
But patiently struggled and waited his time.
He dangled awhile from real poverty's limb,
Yet he got to the top. Was the world against him?

"I could name you a dozen, yes, hundreds, I guess
Of poor boys who've patiently climbed to success;
All boys who were down and who struggled alone,
Who'd have thought themselves rich if your fortune
    They'd known;
Yet they rose in the world you're so quick to condemn,
And I'm asking you now, was the world against them?"

–Edgar A. Guest

One last question to consider. Are you faithful or are you fearful? You can't be both. But you can always decide which attitude you will embrace. Your answer is worth careful consideration.

Applied Faith
by Napoleon Hill

"Faith is the gateway through which one may draw upon Infinite Intelligence."

Faith is a state of mind which has been called "the mainspring of the soul" through which one's aims, desires and plans may be translated into their physical or financial equivalents.

The fundamentals of APPLIED FAITH are these:
- Definiteness of purpose, supported by personal initiative or *action*.
- A positive mental attitude, free from negatives such as envy, hatred, jealousy and fear.
- A "Master Mind" alliance with one or more people who radiate courage based on faith, and who are suited mentally and spiritually to one's needs in carrying out a given purpose.
- Recognition of the fact that every adversity carries with it the seed of an equivalent benefit, that *temporary defeat* is not failure until it has been accepted as such.
- The habit of expressing gratitude for one's blessings daily, in the form of a prayer.

To create a mental attitude favorable for the expression of Applied Faith follow these instructions:
1) Know what you want and determine what you will give in return for it.
2) When you affirm the object of your prayers let your imagination see yourself already in possession of it.
3) Keep your mind open for guidance from within, and when you are inspired by *hunches*, take heed of them immediately for they may bring the answer you seek.

4) When you are overtaken by defeat, as you may be many times, remember that man's faith is often tested in many ways, and defeat may be only your testing time; *therefore accept it only as an inspiration for greater effort.*

There is no such reality as a "blanket" faith. You must have a definite objective, purpose or desire before you can enjoy the benefits of Applied Faith.

Faith is guidance from within which will not bring you that which you seek, but it will show you the path by which you may go after that which you desire.

Faith is the gateway through which you must pass in order to communicate with Infinite Intelligence and draw upon it for help. *And it is the only thing that will make your prayers effective.*

Source: *Success Unlimited.*

GOOD _{AS} GOLD
7

I had two things going for me: my strong work ethic and my ability to "roll with the punches." As Napoleon Hill would say, I had "flexibility." Dr. Hill defines flexibility as "the capacity to adapt one's self to emergencies and rapidly changing circumstances without losing his poise or permitting himself to be thrown off balance through anger."

—Jim Connelly

As an English Major in college, I was assigned to read the short story entitled "Bartleby the Scrivener" by Herman Melville. Melville wrote this work after authoring the classic novel **Moby Dick**. Bartleby was the main character in the story, and he was an unusual one. One day after being employed as a copywriter in a legal office he was given an assignment and his simple response was, "I would prefer not to." Over time, this became his usual rejoinder, much like a mantra. This bewildered everyone, and answers were sought that would explain his behavior. Sadly, the situation worsened, and predictably Bartleby "preferred" himself right out of life. As the story concludes, the reader is forced to wonder why Bartleby decided not to decide. Did he believe his non-decisiveness was creating a safety net around him, or did he feel that by not deciding he was asserting his independence? Whatever his rationale, in the end he was the loser. His lack of deciding self-selected him for extinction.

There are obvious advantages in being flexible. In

decision making flexibility is akin to creative visioning. Being open rather than closed to what the Universe brings to our doorstep places us on the receiving end. Receiving works best as a reciprocal process. To quote St. Francis, "It is in giving that we receive." You give to receive and receive to give. Just as a seed is planted, grows, and is harvested producing more seeds to be planted, your life should do the same. Suppressing this process stunts our growth and hastens our demise. By being flexible, we remain youthful, supple and growing. When we interfere with the process, we begin to deteriorate and die.

Decide not to be rigid, but flexible. Do the unexpected. Take a risk. Accept a challenge. See what the Universe brings to your doorstep. And, who knows? You may just catch a falling star, capture a leprechaun, rub the magic lamp, and really find your pot of gold at the end of the rainbow just as we read about as children. But, you won't do this unless you are flexible enough to reply as winners reply, "Yes, I can!"

Flexibility Can Produce Miracles
by Napoleon Hill

Throughout his long and interesting career, Napoleon Hill has met with, talked with, and studied the world's great. What he has learned from them he passes on to you—along with his own wisdom. Few men in history have been able to influence the lives of so many people for the better as has Napoleon Hill. His writings, among them "Think and Grow Rich," "The Science of Success," and "How to Raise your Own Salary," his lectures, his radio programs and motion pictures have helped countless thousands to help themselves.

Andrew Carnegie, founder of the great United States Steel Corporation, was probably the best judge of men of any industrialist of his time. He was responsible for the success of more men than any other man of his time.

When Mr. Carnegie wanted a man for an important job,

he looked for these traits before hiring him: A keen sense of loyalty—dependability—flexibility—and lastly, ability to do a given job well.

Mr. Carnegie said that if a man was not loyal, dependable, and flexible, no amount of ability could qualify him for a responsible executive or supervisory position. By "flexibility" he meant the capacity to adapt one's self to emergencies and rapidly changing circumstances without losing his poise or permitting himself to be thrown off balance through anger.

He illustrated his point by relating an experience he had with his chief chemist. He wanted the most able chemist that money could hire, so he sent a talent scout to Germany to look for such a man and found him in the employ of the Krupp Gun Works. It took a fabulous salary and a five year contract to break the man away from the Krupp Works, but he was hired and brought to America.

By the end of the first month after the chemist became a member of Mr. Carnegie's master mind group, it became apparent that a mistake had been made in hiring him. The man was, without a doubt, the ablest chemist Mr. Carnegie had ever known, but he had a static, stubborn disposition which made it impossible for other members of the Carnegie organization to get along with him, so he was paid off for the entire five-year contract and dismissed.

One of Mr. Carnegie's executives remarked that this had been a very expensive experience. "Yes," said Carnegie, "but not anywhere near as expensive as it would have been if we had not dismissed him." This was one of the very few times when a man had been chosen for an important position in the Carnegie organizations without having been analyzed by the great industrialist.

The most common of all the causes of individual failure is one's lack of ability to get along with other people. Flexibility cures this weakness. No two people are alike in their personal traits and mental attitudes. The successful person recognizes this fact, and he also recognizes that he cannot make other people over or change their mental attitude to suit his convenience, so *he changes his attitude temporarily* to avoid conflict with others.

We have ears with which to listen and mouths with which to speak, but fortunately we do not have to speak every time we hear something we do not like. Silence can be a powerful weapon, and it is often used by wise people when they are in contact with others who are irritable or inclined to create unpleasant incidents of an argumentative nature.

The late Franklin D. Roosevelt was one of the most flexible men I have ever known. He could be all things to all men with the greatest of ease, and it has been said that this trait of flexibility was his greatest asset and the one thing which made him the most successful politician who ever occupied the White House.

I have seen men come into President Roosevelt's office roaring like lions and after he got through with them they walked out like lambs. One day a very prominent banker came to see the President. He was as mad as a "wet Hen" because a member of the White House staff had kept him waiting what he thought was "too long." Before he was even seated he started right off to air his peeve by saying, "My time's important, and I don't like to have it wasted by flunkies."

Roosevelt turned on that million dollar smile of his and said, "Well, I know just how you feel, for my time is also important, or I am fooling a lot of the people very badly." The caller smiles, apologized to the President, and said, "I would give a million dollars if I had your flexibility." And he probably would have done so gladly.

Hardly a day goes by without experiences in everyone's life which could be blown up to great magnitude of unpleasantness if one does not have the flexibility with which to neutralize them.

There are more than thirty individual traits which, when combined and applied, give one a pleasing personality. Flexibility is a "must" in this group, for without it no one can get along harmoniously with others at all times under all circumstances.

I was destined to learn, during the twenty years of labor I put into the research in organizing my success philosophy, something of the importance of flexibility. I need flexibility on many occasions in order to adjust myself to the need of money. And I needed it in order to convince the five hundred or more top ranking business men and industrialists who collaborated with me in creating the philosophy that their time was wisely spent in helping me.

Flexibility is the answer to almost every unpleasant circumstance with which we meet, and it can best be made to serve during these emergencies if we remember that every adversity *carries with it the seed of an equivalent benefit.* You can very well determine whether or not you have flexibility when adversity overtakes you. If you have it, you will begin at once to look for that "seed of an equivalent benefit" instead of allowing yourself to be thrown off balance by fear, self-pity, anxiety, or resentment.

In order to remain flexible during the early part of the depression which began in 1929, I wrote books. I had no idea of having them published. I wrote merely to maintain my flexibility. However, three of my friends adjusted themselves to the circumstances in a different manner. One of them jumped off a high building, one shot himself to death, and the third "solved" his problem with an overdose of poison. My financial losses due to the depression were as great as those of any of my three friends, but I had one asset which, unfortunately, they did not possess.

One thing I have learned from life's experiences stands out in my mind above all else as a great blessing. I have learned that no experience and no material loss are important to anyone as long as he remains in contact with Infinite Intelligence and keeps sufficient faith in himself to be guided by this Divine source of power. This, too, is flexibility applied, and it often carries convincing evidence that experiences we sometimes regard as irreparable adversities turn out to be blessings instead. For it is true that an all-wise Creator has provided that none may experience a loss of any nature whatsoever without the potential of an equivalent gain in one form or another.

Flexibility gives one the capacity to recognize that whatever the mind can *conceive* and *believe* the mind can *achieve*. And it also gives one the wisdom to recognize that TIME is the great universal healer which can cure most human disappointments and frustrations, and the courage to recognize that strength, physical and spiritual, grows out of struggle.

Source: *Success Unlimited*. September 1955. Vol. II, No. VII. Pgs. 8, 9, 10 & 11.

GOOD ^{AS} GOLD
8

He remembered his army days when he marched under orders of "head up, shoulders back, chest out, stomach in—remember soldier, if you are 6 foot tall, march like you are 6 foot 1." He remembered. He began to walk taller. In reality he lived in the back of a car. Nothing had changed. Except his stammer had disappeared. Strange what a touch of imaginary confidence can do.

—**Michael Johnson**

Trying times can try men's souls. Living a day to day existence without a network of support can put a person on the precarious brink of disaster. Both Napoleon Hill and our guest columnist Michael Johnson have experienced setbacks. More importantly, however, is that they turned their setbacks into victorious comebacks. We've all memorized the saying, "When the going gets tough, the tough get going." This little affirmation reminds us just as Hill's Formula for Self-Confidence reminds us that we must take positive, daily action if we hope to turn the tide of events in our favor.

Bills, relationships, working conditions, living conditions and even the weather can make a sourpuss out of even the Cheshire Cat. You may ask yourself if turning your frown upside down is worth the effort. And, invariably it is. It just so happens that it is the first step in the journey of becoming the comeback kid. Not giving up, never accepting defeat, and not allowing anyone to label you a quitter are the characteristics of a winner. Winners are not losers in the game of life. They are those individuals who practice setting long term goals with persistence, determination, and the desire to go the distance even if it is rocky terrain.

Dr. Hill gives you the formula below in this week's article for developing self-confidence. Read this article with a pen in hand and notebook by your side. If you notice some resemblances to yourself, jot down your thoughts. When you finish, you might just discover why you are not yet on the winner's path. Now that you know the way, why not choose it for yourself? You will be the better for it. Just consider the alternative.

How to Develop Self-Confidence
by Napoleon Hill

"Selling yourself short is effrontery to your Creator."

The greatest person now living is the one who is reading this sentence. If you do not recognize this truth, then you should begin at once to follow these instructions:

- Adopt a Definite Major Purpose and begin where you stand to attain it.
- Write out a clear statement of what you believe to be the advantages of your Definite Major Purpose, and call these into your mind many times daily, in the form of a prayer for their attainment.
- If your Major Purpose is to attain something material, such as money, see yourself already in possession of it when you call it into your consciousness.
- Associate yourself with as many people as possible who are in sympathy with you and your major purpose, and induce them to give you encouragement and faith in every way possible.
- Let not a single day pass without making at least one move toward the attainment of your Definite Major Purpose, and remember that nothing worthwhile is ever

accomplished without ACTION–ACTION–ACTION!

- Choose some prosperous, self-reliant person as your "pace-maker" and make up your mind not only to catch up with him in achievements, *but to excel him.*
- When you meet with defeat, when obstacles get in your way and the going is hard, do not quit, but turn on more will power and keep on keeping on.
- Follow the habit of never running away from disagreeable circumstances, but learn to transmute them into inspiration for achievement of your desires.
- And remember that LOVE and Hate had a falling out. Hate drew a ring around himself that shut LOVE out, but Love got busy with a great big *grin* and *drew a bigger ring that took Hate and his little ring in again.*
- Lastly, recognize the truth that everything worth having has a price one must pay to get it. The price of self-confidence is eternal vigilance in carrying out these instructions. Your watchword must be PERSISTENCY.

And remember, if you sell yourself short through lack of self-confidence you thereby express ingratitude to your Creator, whose one and only exclusive privilege to you is that of mastering and using your own mind for the determination of your own earthly destiny.

Source: *Success Unlimited.*

GOOD AS GOLD
9

Our current economic situation signals opportunity; there is no better time to invest in our future–our children and our students.

–Dr. Frank Frey

When it comes to a Positive Mental Attitude, how do you rate yourself? 5 being excellent and 1 being non-existent, where do you place yourself on the "right mental attitude" continuum of success? Consider for a moment that this self-check on a daily basis might just be the most important part of your mental hygiene necessary for daily renewal regarding your personal belief system. We bathe, comb our hair, brush our teeth, and many more things on a ritual basis, but when it comes to mental scrutiny, oftentimes we may allow ourselves to become unsightly.

I know individuals who not only have memorized Hill's self-confidence formula, but have it taped to their bathroom mirror so that when they are externally preparing for the day ahead, they can also recite the formula and prepare themselves mentally as well as physically through this positive affirmation. Morning is a good time to recite affirmations, self-motivators, or positive thought starters that seep deep into our psyche as we approach the day. A day begun positively helps pre-ordain that the day's outcome will have positive consequences too. Likewise, a day begun thinking about stressful and worrisome concerns also pre-disposes a person for more worry and stress throughout the remainder of the day. The difference between the two is how you pre-determine the standard for your day, for your moment in time on this planet. Only you can choose to color your world in a positive or negative fashion.

Why does all this matter? It matters because in order to become an active participant in the Philosophy of Success, you must first possess the proper mental attitude that is conducive to utilizing the other remaining principles of achievement. Without a positive mental attitude firmly in place, Thomas Edison, Henry Ford, Helen Keller, the Wright brothers, Andrew Carnegie, Napoleon Hill, W. Clement Stone, and their counterparts then and now, would have achieved nothing of lasting consequence. It is with the openness and receptivity of a Positive Mental Attitude firmly in place that your knock on the door of Infinite Intelligence is answered because you expect it to be. Your expectation of success enables the Universe to provide it to you right on schedule after you have taken the appropriate action to bring whatever it is you desire into your world. Consider for a moment how a thought becomes a thing, and how an emotionalized thought becomes a thing even quicker. Now, recall when you desperately wanted something and how you backed it with a positive intention and a good attitude followed through with appropriate action. Most often this object of desire shows up quickly because you know the code or formula for getting things done. It's no secret. It's a success formula composed of attitude, intention, and hard work. Try it and see. It will work every time if you work it!

The Power of a Positive Mental Attitude
by Napoleon Hill

*"Your mental attitude speaks
more loudly than your words."*

A positive mental attitude is the first of the twelve great riches, and it is the means by which you may benefit by the magic power of BELIEVING.

Thomas A. Edison BELIEVED that he could perfect the incandescent electric lamp despite the fact that he failed more than ten thousand times before he made his belief come true.

Marconi BELIEVED that the ether could be made to carry the vibrations of sound without the use of wires and he carried on through many failures until he was rewarded by victory.

Columbus BELIEVED that he would find land in an uncharted ocean and he sailed on and on, despite the threatened mutiny of his sailors, until he found land.

Madam Schuman-Heink BELIEVED that she would become a great singer, although her first teacher advised her to go back to her sewing machine and be contented as a seamstress. Her belief rewarded her with success.

Helen Keller BELIEVED that she would learn to talk despite the fact she had lost the use of speech, sight and hearing, and lived to see that belief provide her with the privilege of serving as a great inspiration to the afflicted all over the world.

Henry Ford BELIEVED that he could build a horseless buggy that would provide low cost rapid transportation, and, despite the farflung cry of "cracked pot" and skepticism of many people, he belted the earth with the product of his belief.

Andrew Carnegie BELIEVED that I could organize a success philosophy based on the "know how" of himself and other successful men, and his belief, transferred to my mind, gave the world the Science of Success which has benefitted huge numbers of people throughout the world.

Our great American Way of Life and our unmatchable system of Free Enterprise are the products of the minds of men who BELIEVED in our system of government and our system of economics.

BELIEVERS are the forerunners of civilization, the builders of industries, the creators of Empires, the revealers of the bountiful benefits made available to us by the Creator of all things.

Source: *Success Unlimited*.

GOOD AS GOLD
10

Communication is like a dance, where we lead and follow, give and receive, speak and listen, create and accept.

–Niurka

The annual Open House at the Napoleon Hill World Learning Center at Purdue University Calumet is generally scheduled during the first two weeks in May. All are welcome to attend. Once you read the listing of daily events, you will agree that this function could not be put on without the Principle of Teamwork. This year's theme is Inspired Authors, Musicians, and Artists who Mirror the Teachings of Dr. Hill. If I do say so myself, the lineup of presenters is outstanding. Indeed there is something for everyone.

Featured authors include Andy Bienkowski and Mary Akers (Radical Gratitude), Rich Winograd (Paloma), Christina Chia (Mind Garden), and Rev. Sam Boys (An Ancient Sound for the Present Moment). Musicians include Antonio Castillo de la Gala (Pianist), Michael Telapary (Flutist), and Rev. Sam Boys, (Didgeridoo Instrumentalist). Artists include Michael Telapary (Artist–Print Design), and Chino Martinez (Labyrinth Creator). A benefit concert with proceeds going to the Chancellor's Scholarship Fund at Purdue University Calumet will occur Tuesday evening, May 5 that features selections played by Antonio, Michael and Sam. Next, an all-day hands-on Didgeridoo workshop for Calumet High School's Band students will occur on Wednesday, May 5 with the public invited to participate.

Finally on Thursday, May 7, the Open House will culminate in a field trip to see "Crazy for You" which is a new musical featuring the works of Gershwin.

And, in between the above events there will be many other opportunities to attend free presentations, network, visit the W. Clement Stone Library, and learn more about the PMA Philosophy of Success as authored by Dr. Napoleon Hill.

Why don't you consider joining us and get on the road to success with a little help from your friends? Our purpose is educating anyone who is interested in bettering themselves by teaching Dr. Hill's Science of Success Philosophy. Isn't it time you invested in your greatest asset–yourself?

Teamwork
by Napoleon Hill

Harmonious cooperation is a priceless asset which you can acquire in proportion to your giving.

Cooperation, like love and friendship, is something you get by giving. There are many travelers on the road that leads to happiness. You will need their cooperation, and they will need yours.

And there will be other generations after ours. Their lot in life will depend largely on the inheritance we leave to them. We must become bridge-builders, not only for the present generation but for generations yet unborn. And we must build for them in the spirit of the old man about whom the poet wrote:

An old man, travelling a lonely highway,
Came at the evening, cold and gray,
To a chasm deep and wide.
The old man crossed in the twilight dim,
For the sullen stream had no fears for him.
But he turned when he reached the other side,

And builded a bridge to span the tide.
"Old man," cried a fellow pilgrim near,
"You are wasting your strength with building here.
Your journey will end with the ending day,
And you never again will pass this way.
"You have crossed the chasm deep and wide.
Why build you a bridge at eventide?"
And the builder raised his old grey head:
"Good friend, on the path I have come," he said,
"There followeth after me today
A youth whose feet must pass this way.
"This stream which has been as naught to me,
To that fair-haired boy may a pitfall be.
He, too, must cross in the twilight dim.
"Good friend, I am building this bridge for him."

This spirit of unselfish team work will provide greater benefits for this generation, as well as help those yet to come. Thus, in serving as bridge-builders for future generations we shall be preparing ourselves for the better things of life which can come only through friendly cooperation.

If you use this philosophy for personal benefit, remember you owe something to those who will follow you. Remember, too, to build for them.

Source: *PMA Science of Success:* Educational Edition. Pgs. 354, 355, & 356.

GOOD AS GOLD
11

But as so wisely it is said, "The teacher appears only when the student is ready."
—Gloria Belendez-Ramirez

When I was teaching high school English, I had a student whose mother gave me a coffee cup with the following saying:

> Each day is a new beginning . . .
> another chance
> to learn more about ourselves,
> to care more about others,
> to laugh more than we did,
> to accomplish more than we thought we could,
> to be more than we were before.
>
> (Author unknown)

Of all the gifts I was given during my tenure as a teacher, this one still means the most to me because it has a story behind it. It is the sentiment and not the gift that makes the cup special.

The student's mother worked in the faculty cafeteria where I taught, but I never connected the worker with one of my students because I only knew her by her first name. One day while going through the cafeteria line, I was praising a student's work and indicated that even though he was taking the class for the second time during a summer session in order to graduate on schedule, his work was exceptional. I doubted that he lacked talent or initiative to do the work. Perhaps, Michael wasn't motivated previously. Now, however, his motivation and work were at the top of the class.

As I talked on and on I knew that I was praising this young man but it didn't matter because we were all colleagues and interested in the performance of our students. It only troubled me a little to think back when just a few weeks ago I was cautioned by his counselor that he would be nothing but trouble in the class, and ultimately a failure. I guess that I was singing his praises because just the opposite happened and he was a strong participant and good contributor in the class. If truth be told, I was glad that he was in the class and that the counselor's prediction of trouble never happened. I was relieved and grateful to the young man for working so diligently.

When I approached the cash register to pay, the woman taking my money said just two words–"Thank you." Somehow, I knew it wasn't for my lunch payment, so I asked, "For what?" She simply looked at me and said, "Michael is my son and you are the first teacher to ever say anything good about him." I was stunned. I said I had no idea. I stumbled over my words quickly repeating that he was good in class, no problem at all, and was earning a high grade. Again, I justified his positive performance, and she just listened and took it all in–as any proud mother would.

In a significant way, I felt that she had won a victory that day in front of the counselor and other teachers in the lunchroom. After I finished defending Michael, she told me that Michael performed because it was expected of him to perform in my class. Others did not have a high expectation for him, therefore he chose to do little, nothing, or cause a disruption.

So, you see the teacher learned a great deal from her student and also from the mother behind the student. She knew that positive expectations lead to positive performance. And, she later gave me the cup to remind me that each day is a new beginning–not just for us, but for the people we encounter. In this throw-a-way society, it matters when we identify and praise openly a hidden gem of talent that to others may only seem like garbage. The difference lives forever in the life of the one who unearthed the jewel and also to the person who realizes that the gem of talent is inside of him and he only has to polish it to perfect it.

That's why I keep the cup. I never want to forget the lesson or the student who taught it to me. When hidden talent is unearthed the entire world becomes the better for it.

The Difference Between Wishing and Believing
by Napoleon Hill

The majority of people never discover the difference between wishing and believing; nor do they recognize that there are six steps which people usually follow in using their mind-power for the attainment of their desires. These steps are:

First: The vast majority of people go through life by merely *wishing* for things. The percentage of people who stop at *wishing* is estimated at: 70%

Second: A much smaller percentage of the people develop their wishes into *desires*. These are estimated at: 10%

Third: A still smaller percentage of the people develop their wishes and desires into *hopes*. These are estimated at: 8%

Fourth: A still smaller percentage of the people step their mind-power up to where it becomes *belief*. These are estimated at: 6%

Fifth: And yet a very much smaller percentage of the

people crystallize wishes, desires and hopes into belief, and then into *burning desire,* and finally *faith.* This percentage is estimated at: 4%

Sixth: And last, a very small percentage of the people take the last two steps, putting *their faith into action by (1) planning and (2) acting to carry out their plans.* This percentage is estimated at only: 2%

The outstanding leaders in every walk of life are the ones in the sixth group. They recognize the power of their own minds, take possession of that power and direct it to whatever ends they choose. To these people the word *impossible* has no meaning. To them *everything* they want or need is *possible* and they manage to get it. The only trait which differentiates them from most of the others who accept failure as their lot, is that they recognize and use their mind-power for the attainment of the circumstances and things they want while the others do not.

Source: *PMA Science of Success.* Pgs. 232 & 233.

GOOD ᴬˢ GOLD
12

The ties that bind can also be the ties that blind.
Stay loving and optimistic, but keep your eyes open
even when dealing with those closest to you.
— **Eliezer A. Alperstein, CPA**

As each of us climbs the success ladder it is only a matter of time until we stumble on a loose rung or two. At that precise moment we either stabilize ourselves preventing a nasty fall or lose our footing. Life is like that too. Things can be moving along in the right direction, and then without notice something happens that upsets our equilibrium or foothold on life. It can be as simple as a bad commute to work, or as life changing as a death in the family. Each occurrence does contribute to our level of stress and thereby impacts our overall performance. When these shakeups occur, how does a person rebound and continue to perform at a high level?

Napoleon Hill would answer the above question by telling everyone that they should never forego their positive mental attitude. Having a positive attitude is good insurance that you will come back from the adversity and not forfeit any ground that you have gained. With a positive mental attitude you are conditioning your mind for success, even in the throes of despair. I always remember W. Clement Stone's statement "God is always a good God." Even with the loss of his two eldest children, Stone never cursed God demanding to know why it happened. Rather, he stated consistently that the nature of God was goodness, and therefore the Creator intended no harm. Stone knew this for a fact and his unquestionable belief demonstrated to the world the power of a positive mental attitude.

A person's willingness to look on the bright side of life even while overcoming difficulties does not make him feeble-minded or naïve. Rather, this inclination to forecast good even while experiencing bad underscores and heightens the value of optimism. Expecting goodness conditions us for goodness and makes us seek it out. The opposite, unfortunately, is also true. Napoleon Hill states that "You are where you are because of your habits of thought." Thought just like action can be a habit. Do you have a habit of thinking positive or negative thoughts? Is your thought habit something you should cultivate or give up? Of course, you are free to choose just as you are with other habits. And, in the choosing we are determining our destiny. Ask yourself, "What future are my thoughts foretelling?" Only you can predict that outcome. If, as they say, it's in the cards, you obviously have stacked the deck for or against yourself by your attitude of choice.

A Man's Mental Attitude
by Napoleon Hill

A man's mental attitude in respect to defeat is the factor of major importance in determining whether he rides with the tides of fortune on the success side of the River of Life or is swept to the failure side by circumstances of misfortune.

The circumstances which separate failure from success often are so slight that their real cause is overlooked. Often they exist entirely in the mental attitude with which one meets temporary defeat. The man with a positive mental attitude reacts to defeat in a spirit of determination not to accept it. The man with a negative mental attitude reacts to defeat in a spirit of hopeless acceptance.

The man who maintains a positive mental attitude may have anything in life upon which he may set his heart, so long as it does not conflict with the laws of God and the rights of his fellowmen. He probably will experience many defeats, but he will not surrender to defeat. He will convert it into a stepping stone from which he will rise to higher and higher areas of achievement.

The subject of a positive mental attitude is so important that it not only claimed first position in the list of the twelve riches of life, but it had to be included as an important part of the principle on pleasing personality, and has been mentioned in practically every principle of this course.

A positive mental attitude is an essential part of the key which unlocks the door to the solution of all personal problems. It is the magic quality of this key which enables it to attract success as surely as an electro-magnet attracts iron filings.

The whole secret of the formula by which you may turn defeat into an asset lives in your ability to maintain a positive mental attitude despite your defeat.

This is no man-made rule. It is a part of the imponderable phenomena of nature through which man has been provided with the privilege of drawing upon that power known as faith. Faith and a positive mental attitude are twin brothers! Where one is found, there also will be the other. The two are inseparable. Faith is a power which cannot be analyzed by science, yet it is the greatest power available to mankind.

And the strangest of its qualities exists in the fact that it is free, equally available to the humblest person or the greatest. Recognize this truth and you will be well on your way toward the great estate of Happy Valley.

Source: *PMA Science of Success.* Pgs. 396 & 397.

GOOD AS GOLD
13

A goal will cause you to get up early, pursue its outcome with a passion, look for other solutions when obstacles arise, and seek the help of others in order to reach your goal.

–Don M. Green

At this time of year, I recall Emerson saying that the earth laughs in flowers. What a beautiful poetic image of springtime. The rebirth of the earth during this season causes one to pause and wonder where all this beauty comes from after the cold and frozen months of winter. In one of Dylan Thomas's early poems, he credits a spiritual essence with the beauty that erupts from the seemingly dead earth as he states "The force that through the green fuse drives the flower." This force, no doubt, is the Infinite Intelligence that Dr. Hill continually makes reference to in his teachings. As with the earth, it is this force that has created us too. Remember, we are a part of nature that we find ourselves in–not apart from it.

When you consider how we as humans achieve desired outcomes, Dr. Hill reminds us that it is always in our best interests to align our goals with the natural laws of nature. He reminds us that we are inside a system that was created by Infinite Intelligence. This design plan is the Operations Manual of the Universe and if we are to be successful, we must always stay in code, or, in other words, stay in synchronization with the laws of nature.

Napoleon Hill states: "Nature yields her most profound

secrets to the man who is determined to uncover them." This gentle reminder of how persistence is the key to solving the mysteries of the Universe brings us back full circle to the idea that a Force or a Spirit is responsible for our existence in the world in which we live. Therefore, it makes perfect sense to align ourselves to the natural laws of the Universe when we seek to accomplish anything.

By setting goals in accordance with the natural laws and creative force that enables a flower to blossom we are working within the natural order of things. For some people, this alignment never occurs because they believe themselves to be exempt from the rules of order. Their goals either have an early demise or never come to fruition because they do not follow the established path.

As you learn how to set and achieve workable goals, know that it is easier if you align your goals with your overall definite major purpose and corresponding talents. Take a thorough inventory first of your assets to be certain that you possess essential skills and capabilities to match your desired area of personal growth. This is not to say that everything must be in place before you start, just the basic components. Then, get to work in doing whatever it is you have to do to make your goal manifest in reality through persistent action accompanied with strong faith in a positive outcome. This is a good foundation on which to build. Now, read the following suggestions from Dr. Hill in living your purpose by inching up the ladder of success one accomplished goal at a time.

A Lesson From Nature
by Napoleon Hill

Everything, animate or inanimate, starts out as a nucleus–a whirling bit of energy which, although so small as to defy the lens of the microscope, has the power to attract to itself whatever of a like nature it requires for its sustenance and growth.

Remember the acorn and the handful of earth. Locked up within that acorn is the germ of life, the nucleus which is capable of drawing from its surrounding elements of soil, air, water, and sunlight, the materials to build an oak tree.

Take a seed of corn or wheat; plant it in the ground and it will create a center of activity which attracts from its environment the precise balance of chemical constituents which will produce a cornstalk, or a stalk of wheat, and bring forth a reproduction of itself, according to the law of growth and increased returns.

These analogies help us to get a true picture of the power of the mind through self-suggestion. You can see how it is possible to sow a seed of desire with the subconscious mind through conscious expressed repetition of this desire . . . to feed and nourish this seed by the stimulus of high emotion . . . to germinate it by the sunshine of faith, and thus to attract to yourself from the bounteous supply of life energy in Infinite Intelligence the practical plans whereby that original seed of desire may be developed into its physical counterpart.

The law of attraction is based upon the principle of growth from the vitality which is inherent in the seed (idea or desire) itself. Every seed has a potentially perfect plant. Every worthy desire has in it the potential power for its perfect fulfillment. If a seed is to germinate and produce a crop after its own kind, it must be planted in fertile soil, it must have nourishment, and it must have sunshine to ripen it for harvest.

Your subconscious mind can be compared to a fertile garden spot wherein may be planted the seed of your definite purpose, by means of a burning desire which imparts the initial energy into the nucleus of your definite purpose, and causes it to enlarge and grow. Now we have explained how the seed may be nourished and cultivated by persistent action according to your plans and through repeated instructions to your subconscious. Also how you may attract the vitalizing influence of Infinite Intelligence and focus it on the object of your desire. Here you have the whole process laid before you. It is a process which is going on all around you in countless forms of life. It is not a matter of theory. It is a demonstrated fact. You have only to adapt it to your own definite purpose.

Source: *PMA Science of Success*. Pgs. 106 & 107.

GOOD AS GOLD
14

When the mind is clear of clutter, we can set our intention and move toward decisive action. This is the power of Presence.

–Dr. Sam Boys

The Power of Concentration places us at the door of infinite possibilities, but only if we take action to enter the threshold and walk through to our future. No amount of visioning and anticipation will replace the required action that determines our outcome. We attract what we think about all day long, but not as if by magic–but by effort, self-discipline, accurate thinking, controlled attention, and systematic work. Old-fashioned work grounds our creative visioning and links the thought to the product. You might look at it as a continuum of timing that begins with the kernel of an idea (thought) and ends with a tangible product due to action taken (outcome).

I have seen a planted vision take hold of an individual's awareness and result in a product that mirrors the creative thought. Just recently I was able to watch a dream fulfilled. I was in the presence of Rev. Sam Boys as he logged on to Amazon.com and saw the book he had just published appear on the screen for the first time. It was timeless, and a cherished moment for him as he viewed *An Ancient Sound for the Present Moment* appearing as a product of his heart's desire. Just a few months prior, Sam said that he had not written a book on the meditative practices of the didgeridoo and I encouraged him to do so. Now it was not only written but available for the world to read. He took the seed of an idea–a thought–and decided to make it so! And, the outcome is wonderful. Sam will be performing at our open house on May 5th and 6th, Tuesday and Wednesday for both students and adults. Why not come and witness his dream fulfilled?

Also, artist Michael Telapary and concert pianist Antonio Castillo de la Gala have grabbed hold of two thoughts that are coming to fruition as well for our open house. Michael has created a series of remarkable images to correspond to the 17 Success Principles, and Antonio has produced an instrumental CD of piano music that link to the 17 Success Principles as well. Finally, my executive assistant, Chino Martinez, is capitalizing on an idea to produce a photo publication depicting his experiences with creating labyrinths around the world. What a wealth of ideas from only seeds of thought!

What do all these authors, artists, and musicians have to do with you? Everything. If one person can do it, Dr. Hill states that we all can do it. Sam, Mike, Antonio, and Chino have accepted the challenge and created a remarkable outcome, and you can too! What is your personal dream? What aspiration keeps tugging at your sleeve? What keeps you up at night and won't loosen its grip on your creative imagination? That, my friend, is your challenge–your future in the making. It's that seed of thought that Napoleon Hill tells you to act on quickly because it is a gift from the Universe and it has your name on it. Will you open it and show it to the world? Your dream awaits . . . and the world is waiting too.

The Power of Concentration
by Napoleon Hill

Concentration on one's major purpose projects a clear picture of that purpose upon the conscious mind and holds it there until it is taken over by the subconscious and acted upon. This is called controlled attention.

Controlled attention is the act of coordinating all the faculties of the mind and directing their combined power to a given end. It is an act which can be achieved only by the strictest sort of self-discipline. Attention that is not controlled and directed may be nothing more than idle curiosity. The word controlled is the key to thought power.

You may achieve controlled attention by the application of the following six factors, through the application of self-discipline:

a) Definiteness of purpose, the starting point of all achievement.

b) Imagination, through which the object of one's purpose is illuminated and mirrored in the mind so clearly that its nature cannot be mistaken.

c) Desire, turned on until it becomes burning desire that will not be denied.

d) Faith in the ultimate achievement of your purpose. This faith must be so strong that you can already see yourself in possession of the object of your definite major purpose.

e) Will-power, applied continuously, in full force, in support of faith.

f) The subconscious mind picks up the picture conveyed to it by the foregoing factors and carries it to its logical conclusion by whatever practical means may be available, according to the nature of your purpose.

Effective concentration, or controlled attention, then requires that your attention be fully controlled and directed toward a definite end. Controlled attention is the highest form of self-discipline.

Thus it is obvious that all the previously mentioned principles of this philosophy blend with, and become a part of, the principle of controlled attention. If you have mastered these previous principles, and have followed the instructions given, you are now ready to take complete charge of your mind power and direct it to whatever ends you desire, with reasonable assurance that you will not fail.

It is not the intent of this philosophy to suggest to any one the nature of the purpose or objective which he should desire. The Creator has provided every person with the privilege of directing his thoughts and desires to ends of his own choice. Therefore reason and common sense impel us to follow that example.

We can state, however, with emphasis born of great faith, that controlled attention places one on the road to achieving the master-key to the power of the mind. It is a scientific method of contacting and drawing upon Infinite Intelligence for the supply of all human needs. We believe in these truths because we have seen them demonstrated under a great variety of circumstances.

Controlled attention is organized mind power!

When it is applied as prayer, controlled attention gives you direct contact with the Source of all power. This is an inescapable conclusion and has the hearty support of every accurate thinker.

Source: *PMA Science of Success* Educational Edition. Pgs. 332 & 333.

GOOD ᴬˢ GOLD
15

Good thoughts and actions can never produce bad results; bad thoughts and actions can never produce good results. You will reap what you sow. This is a Law of Nature.

–Christina Chia

Remember the nursery rhyme "Mary, Mary quite contrary? How does you garden grow?" Little did we realize as children that what we plant in the earth grows in the same manner as what we plant in our subconscious minds. Why doesn't someone equate seeds of thought with zinnia seeds or watermelon seeds that we plant in our flower and vegetable gardens as soon as the last frost has passed? The minute the holidays are over we receive seed catalogues in the mail and we aspire to grow the largest Big Boy tomatoes and the perfect peace rose, so why can't we dream and visualize exactly what we want to grow in our Mind Garden as well? It's not really that difficult. Through visualization, the creation of a plan, and then by taking the required corresponding actions, we are able to materialize what we once nurtured as a seed of thought in our mind's secret subconscious garden.

This week Christina Chia will present her newest book *Mind Garden* at our annual Open House. Her book is a beautiful compilation of colorful photos of actual flower gardens that mirror the beauty of a person's highest thoughts. Christina convincingly presents the idea that a seed of thought that germinates, grows, and matures will result in a beautiful outcome that can be harvested. Dreams can and do become reality if we learn how to ground them in the here and now.

Why not share this idea with a child? If children can memorize and recite nursery rhymes that stay with them for a lifetime, they can easily learn to program their subconscious minds for success using the same memory tools. Affirmations, self-confidence formulas, action plans, and commands such as "Do it now!" assist those of us who are convinced that these techniques predispose us to positive outcomes.

Share these secrets with young people who are ready to begin their life's gardens. You can be the master gardener who sets the vision for a positive life outcome just by using the gardening metaphor. Life can be a garden. Life began in a garden. Why not demonstrate to a child how to use the tools they have been given to grow their life's garden exactly to their specifications? If you plant ideas, you will become immortal. Physically, you will not live forever, but your ideas will in the hearts and minds of those who follow your lead, and that's how your life goes on. It might just be the time and place to get it right for those who come after you. It's Spring. Plant a garden. Better yet, plant two. One garden in the plot of your choice, and the other garden in the fertile soil of a young person's mind. Both harvests will be worth the wait.

Have You Planted Your Garden with Weeds???
by Napoleon Hill

You succeed in bringing to a natural and logical conclusion whatever thought you permit to dominate your mind. If you harvest a crop of poverty, sickness and disharmony, it is because you have allowed the negative seeds of such thoughts to become imbedded in the soil of your subconscious mind. They have multiplied and brought forth fruit after their own kind. The law is operating in its natural, orderly fashion, but, unfortunately, you have planted the garden with weeds.

Take a look at the vacant lots in your neighborhood, or at unplowed fields: there, every spring, you will find a tremendous crop of fine, lovely, full-grown weeds. The seeds for these weeds have blown to these uncultivated places and automatically, assisted only by natural sunshine and moisture, have taken root and grown. No one has taken the time to dig them up and plant more desirable crops. And that's exactly what happens to the average person who drifts aimlessly through life, without making up his mind as to what he wants. Seeds of all sorts of thoughts (weeds) drop into the soil of his subconscious from all the influences which he encounters in his environment, and he never takes the time to sort out the good from the bad, the desirable from the undesirable, and to eliminate all that is not desirable and replace it with a definite objective which he craves with a burning desire. Thus the weeds take over, and he never produces a worthwhile crop.

Your mind is never idle. It works all the time. It's up to you to put it to work producing the things you want, rather than letting it run wild, attracting things you don't want.

But once you have made up your mind to do something definite, adversities will still come along to prevent you from being successful, if they can. These are simply to test your faith. The more testing your faith endures, the stronger and durable it will become. When such temporary defeats come, accept them as inspiration for greater effort and determination on your part. Carry on with the belief that you will succeed.

Source: *PMA Science of Success.* Pgs. 108 & 109.

GOOD AS GOLD
16

The Success System That Never Fails - *I thought it was a book on how to sell life insurance and stuck it in our bookcase at home. It wouldn't remain there. The next weekend the book fell off the shelf onto the floor. I picked it up and saw these words:* **What the mind can conceive and believe, the mind can achieve...Thought is the most tremendous force in the universe...you become what you think!**

—John Randolph Price

W. Clement Stone was born over a century ago on May 4, 1902 to Louis and Anna M. (Gunn) Stone. By the age of three he was fatherless and raised in a household where he and his mother lived with relatives. From this all too unfortunate beginning, Stone grew up miraculously to become a gentleman who typified the main character in the Horatio Alger "rags to riches" success stories that he read as a youngster. These stories assisted Stone in developing a definite major purpose for his life. He states, "All I want to do is change the world."

Rooted strongly in his belief that he could achieve his dreams because of his thoughts, Stone knew that a Positive Mental Attitude would take him far in life although he did not have a name for this process at the time. He worked diligently to change his situation by changing his thoughts and pattern of thinking.

At the age of six working as a newspaper boy on the South Side of Chicago selling the Examiner, he realized that if he was to be competitive in an aggressive market, he had to be persistent, self-disciplined, courageous and enthusiastic enough to carve out his own niche before he could begin to compete in an established territory run by older boys who were not only competitive but cruel.

Stone's life is a story deserving to be told and recognized. Throughout his 100 years, he personified the individual who recognized that success depended upon certain characteristics that enabled one to achieve success no matter what the circumstances. He developed a simple formula that he called R2A2 and this formula for success was a combination of the acquired information that he culled from reading and reflecting on current success materials as well as his own sharp intuition and insight. The initials and numbers in the formula stand for the words Recognize, Relate, Assimilate, and Apply. Termed a thought starter and a self-affirming command, Stone capitalized on this reminder as he worked daily to learn all he could about the business he was in at the time. His existence turned into a lifetime of shared riches as he struggled to become the ideal that he read about and fashioned from all the childhood literary models he acquired through the Horatio Alger books.

Stone's first example of success was his mother and for this one special gift from God he was always grateful. His mother was typical yet unique, hard-working, yet caring, focused on an independent life with her only son, yet knowing that she had to work long hours to make this happen because she alone had to do it. From his early years Stone was raised in a run-down neighborhood in Chicago's South Side. Easily he could have become a product of his environment as bad company and negative habits were capable of establishing patterns that could condition a person for a lifetime of failure.

Sensing that her son was on the wrong path and that he was acquiring habits such as smoking cigarettes, playing hookey from school, and hanging around with bad companions that would not serve him well in his young adult life, Stone's mother decided to enroll him in a parochial boarding school at Nauvoo, Illinois for the purpose of bettering his environment through exposure to more wholesome living. Once attending and living at this school, Stone became acquainted with the qualities of character that he adopted for his entire life. He states that, "As the weeks passed into months and months into years, I developed a secret ambition to be like my religious father–the pastor whom I admired and loved." The guidance that Anna Stone prayed for with her son was granted and it was at the Spaulding Institute that he was introduced to the three ingredients of the success system that never fails and his life began to spike upward because he recognized that something happened and it was good. Rather than becoming embittered because of being sent away to boarding school, Stone recognized the seed of an equivalent advantage in the temporary adversity of being separated from his mother, and determined to make the best of the situation.

Cosmic Habitforce:
The Law Which Fixes All Habits
by Napoleon Hill

Man is the only living creature equipped with the power of choice through which he may establish his own thought and behavior patterns, or habits, or break them and rearrange them at will.

But while the Creator has given man the privilege of controlling his thoughts, He has also subjected man to the law of cosmic habitforce through which his thought habits must invariably clothe themselves in their physical likeness and equivalent. Cosmic habitforce does not dictate what thoughts a man must express, but it takes over whatever he does think and do, and sees to it that man's thoughts and actions go on to fulfill the measure of their creation.

If a man's dominating thoughts are of poverty, the law

77

translates these thoughts into physical terms of misery and want. But if a man's dominating thoughts are of happiness and contentment, peace of mind and material wealth, the law transforms them into their physical counterpart. Man builds the pattern through his dominating thoughts, while the law of cosmic habitforce casts the mold according to the patterns man develops.

It is very evident that this great law of nature does not make something of nothing. Cosmic habitforce works in harmony with all other laws of nature, such as those of motion, gravity, electricity, magnetism, universal gravitation and the like. But it is greater than all or any of these because it is the very power under which they all operate.

The other natural laws are each a different manifestation of Infinite Intelligence at work, expressing itself in accordance with fixed habits of action and reaction.

The orderliness of the world gives evidence that all natural laws are under the control of a universal plan.

How does cosmic habitforce convert a positive emotion or desire created in the mind of man into its physical equivalent? It intensifies that emotion or desire until it induces that state of mind known as faith. In this state the mind becomes receptive to the inflow of Infinite Intelligence from whence are derived perfect plans to be followed by the individual for the attainment of his desired objective. These plans are always carried out by natural means.

Cosmic habitforce does not directly transmute desires for money into the coin of the realm, but it does activate the imagination to reveal to the individual a way to make the conversion though accepted procedure. This force works no miracles, makes no attempt to create something out of nothing. It helps, or rather–compels, the creator of a strong desire to carry his thoughts to completion through all possible and available natural media.

Source: *PMA Science of Success Course* Pgs. 492 & 493.

GOOD AS GOLD
17

Always remember that in business, if you're not in the mood to take care of your clients, there's always someone else that will be happy to do it for you.
            —Tony Johnson

Having a talent for sewing, Anna Stone worked to establish herself as an expert seamstress. She trained herself to design, fit, and sew for exclusive clientele and developed a following by working at a ladies' establishment know as Dillon's in Chicago. Earning good money she next was able to move to her own apartment in a better neighborhood. About this same time Stone begged his mother to allow him to return home to live with her permanently. He was ready, homesick, and certain that this new environment would not pose the problems that they encountered in the old run-down neighborhood. She agreed and they became a family once again after living apart for over two years.

Reflecting on his time at the boarding school, Stone relates that this is where he developed his inspiration to action. As he watched the religious community that cared for his well-being strive to perfect themselves and others, he realized that this drive toward self-improvement was a worthy effort and capable of changing his life for the better. He then reasoned that this principle—inspiration to action—was the cornerstone of his philosophy of belief in self-improvement, and right then and there he used the first part of his R2A2 formula for himself. He recognized and acknowledged the significance of being inspired to take action because of the worthy goal of self-improvement. He fondly states in consideration of this new found awareness, "The best thoughts that are new are the best thoughts that are old." Spaulding Institute gave Stone the drive and inspiration that he needed to kick-start his life and next make the life he was given his own magnificent obsession.

Next, the second part of his three part success formula was now coming into focus. Stone realized that he had to amass the know-how or knowledge that would allow him to make this happen. Looking back on his early success at selling newspapers as a youngster at the incredible age of six years old, he remembered what happened on that fateful day at Hoelle's Restaurant. This one incident was the starting point of his entire career and it positioned Stone for his lifetime of success. In his own words, he recalls the incident.

> *I was six years old and scared. Selling newspapers on Chicago's tough South Side wasn't easy, especially with the older kids taking over the busy corners, yelling louder, and threatening me with clenched fists. The memory of those dim days is still with me, for it's the first time I can recall turning a disadvantage into an advantage. It's a simple story, unimportant now . . . and yet it was a beginning.*
>
> *Hoelle's Restaurant was near the corner where I tried to work, and it gave me an idea. It was a busy and prosperous place that presented a frightening aspect to a child of six. I was nervous, but I walked in hurriedly and made a lucky sale at the first table. Then diners at the second and third tables bought papers. When I started for the fourth, however, Mr. Hoelle pushed me out the front door.*
>
> *But I had sold three papers. So when Mr. Hoelle wasn't looking, I walked back in and called at the fourth table. Apparently, the jovial customer liked my gumption; he paid for the paper and gave me an extra dime before Mr. Hoelle pushed me out once again. But I had already*

sold four papers and got a "bonus" dime besides. I walked into the restaurant and started selling again. There was a lot of laughter. The customers were enjoying the show. One whispered loudly, "Let him be," as Mr. Hoelle came toward me. About five minutes later, I had sold all my papers.

This know-how or information acquired through taking action became the second part of the Stone's success formula. Know-how is acquired by trial and error followed by personal reflection as to what worked and what didn't work. As Stone was acquiring the knowledge that he used as his working capital for future investments in himself, Anna Stone was broadening her horizons as well. Backed by two years of being an exceptional seamstress at Dillon's, Anna decided to open her own dressmaking business. She did so, and hired two full time employees to assist her. She worked hard and tirelessly at her new role, but financial problems still plagued her family and business.

Once sensing her frustration and worried nature, Stone decided to do something nice for his mother and withdrew a huge amount from his savings account that he established with the proceeds from his newspaper route. He spent a substantial portion of his lifetime savings on a dozen of the most beautiful long stemmed roses that he could find and presented them to his mother in recognition for all the good things she had done for him. She was elated at the special gift for "no reason" and recalled the story many times over her lifetime. It was one of those special moments that money couldn't buy or replace, yet Stone stated that: "This experience made me realize that money was a good thing to have–for the good it could do."

Take Inventory of Yourself
by Napoleon Hill

And now we bring you to that portion of this philosophy

which calls for a careful personal inventory on your part in order to determine how much of your time you are using wisely and beneficially, and how much of it you are wasting. This inventory requires that you answer (to yourself) these questions:

a. Do you have a definite major purpose, and if so, how much of your time are you devoting to attaining that purpose?

b. If you have such a purpose, what plan or plans have you for its attainment? Are you working your plans persistently, through organized effort, or working them only intermittently, when the notion strikes you?

c. Is your definite major purpose obsessional, or is it merely a wish or a weak hope?

d. What have you planned to give in return for the realization of the object of your definite major purpose?

e. What steps have you taken to associate yourself with others, under the master mind principle, for the attainment of your purpose?

f. Have your formed the habit of accepting temporary defeat as a challenge to great effort?

g. Which is the stronger, your faith in the attainment of the object of your definite major purpose, or your fear that you may not attain it?

h. To which do you devote more time: the carrying out of the plan you have adopted for the attainment of your major purpose, or brooding over the obstacles you may have to overcome to attain it?

i. Are you willing to forego personal pleasures temporarily so that you may have more time to devote to the attainment of your major purpose, and are you doing so?

j. Do you recognize the truth that you have no assurance of more than one second of time–this very second–in which to live; that your life is being measured out to you second by second; that once a second has passed it can never be recalled, and the use you make of it can never be changed or modified?

k. Do you recognize that the present circumstances of your life are the result of the use you have made of your time in the past; that this very second may through its proper use, change the entire course of your life?

l. Do you recognize that your mental attitude, whether it is positive or negative, can be changed at will in one second of time?

m. Do you know of any way in which you can be sure of personal success except by the use you make of your time, through the thoughts you think and the physical action with which you back those thoughts through organized plans?

n. Do you believe you will ever succeed by luck or by some unexpected good fortune which is not related to your own thoughts and deeds?

o. Do you know any person who is apt to inspire you with the necessary personal initiative to enable you to attain the object of your major purpose unless you take the lead and first inspire yourself?

p. When you are overtaken by defeat, do you analyze its

cause and determine why it happened, or look for some plausible alibi with which to explain it?

q. Do you believe there is a natural law through the operation of which every individual is forced to benefit, or suffer, from the results of his own thoughts and deeds?

r. Finally, are you accepting a part of this philosophy and rejecting other parts? Or, are you applying the entire philosophy, according to the instructions given, in all of your thoughts and deeds?

These are questions you must answer if you are to take a firm hold of yourself and make the best use of your time. They are direct questions and some of them are very personal, while others are almost brutally blunt. But they are the questions which every successful man must answer at one time or another.

Source: *PMA Science of Success.* Pgs. 479, 480, & 481.

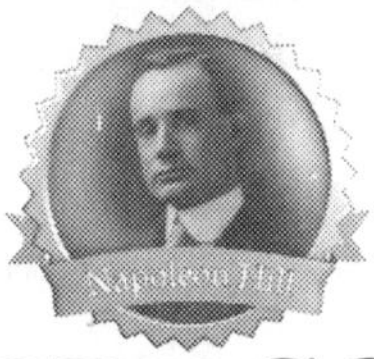
Napoleon Hill

GOOD AS GOLD 18

Our greatest difficulties bring us, simultaneously, our greatest pain and our greatest possibilities to develop as human beings, or as Dr. Hill said in a different way, "Every adversity carries with it the seed of an equivalent benefit."

–Eliezer A. Alperstein

Yet again on another occasion, Stone wanted to recognize his mother's January 6th birthday in a special way, but funds were low due to Christmas spending. He had less than a single dollar in his bank account. As he walked the streets of Chicago he prayed for guidance regarding the gift. Returning home from school at lunchtime, he next heard ice cracking beneath his feet. He continued to travel homeward, but something inside spoke to him and said "Go back." He listened to this interior voice, retraced his steps, and glancing down he noticed a crumpled piece of green paper. Picking it up, he was amazed to find a ten-dollar bill. Excited, he hurried home to make a handwritten birthday note and instead of a gift, he placed the note and the money underneath his mother's plate so that she would find it when she cleared the table. She was delighted with the gift from her only son, but more delighted with the thought that accompanied it. For W. Clement Stone, these two early exercises in gift giving transferred into a lifetime of gratitude and an unparalleled history of philanthropy.

He summarized the lesson this way:

When an adult makes a decision, it is likely to be

foolish or sound, depending on his past experiences in coming to decisions. For the little things that are good ripen into big things that are good. And the little things that are bad ripen into big things that are bad. And this applies to decisions.

But good decisions must be followed through with action. Without action, a good decision becomes meaningless, for the desire itself can die through lack of an attempt to achieve its fulfillment. That's why you should act immediately on a good decision.

This completes the third part of the three step success formula for Stone.

The steps are: 1) Inspiration to Action, 2) Know-how, and 3) Activity Knowledge. These steps works in tandem with the R2A2 formula for getting what you want out of life–Recognize, Relate, Assimilate, and Apply. Stone learned what works through basic trial and error. In his *Success System that Never Fails* he details these very same steps for you too.

Stone's early beginnings fortified him for a life of work and success. After grammar school, Stone attended Senn High School. He boarded with an English family because his mother was required to move to Detroit in order to pursue a business investment with a small insurance agency that represented the United States Casualty Company. Mrs. Stone invested everything she had in this agency, including two pawned diamonds, but her first day of running her own business left her without a single sale. Stone recalls his mother stating:

"I was desperate. I had invested all the cash I had, and I just had to get my money's worth out of this investment. I had tried my best, but I hadn't made a sale. That night I prayed for guidance. And the next morning, I prayed for guidance. When I left home, I went to the largest bank in the city of Detroit. There I sold a policy to the cashier and got permission to sell in the bank during working hours. It seemed that within me there was a driving force that was so sincere that all obstacles were removed. That day I made 44 sales."

Witnessing his mother's determination to succeed no matter what, Stone began to follow in her footsteps. During holidays and summer vacations, Stone would stay with his mother in Detroit. There he learned to sell accident insurance and began the creation of his success system that would never fail him for life. As he honed his system of approaching and connecting with the customer, his expertise and sales increased exponentially. Soon, he could no longer afford to stay in school because he had too much potential income to lose. As a consequence of his success, he dropped out of high school to pursue a career together with his mother in insurance sales.

Try as he might, even when returning to night school after earning his high school diploma at a later date he still was not able to keep up the steady pace that school work coupled with insurance sales demanded. He had to forfeit one or the other, and because of Stone's desire to succeed in the insurance business, sales always won his time, but not totally his heart. W. Clement Stone grew in wisdom through continued reading and self-instruction. He loved learning and pursued many subjects outside of the classroom to further his personal education. His library alone shows his love for reading. Not only did he own and index volumes of material in his personal library, he read and annotated these volumes as well. Never becoming the attorney that he dreamed about, he nevertheless went on to sponsor other individuals to achieve their dreams of a higher education coupled with a degree. Stone never stood by the sidelines and watched things happen. He made them happen–if not for himself then for others.

On a personal note, Stone always remembered his mother with much love. In his famous essay that appeared frequently in *Success Unlimited,* Stone recalls his wife placing a Christmas Card from his mother on the breakfast table one Christmas morning. Seeing his name, Clement, written in his mother's handwriting caused him to pause. How is this possible? Stone's mother was gone now for some time. While enjoying the miracle of a special Christmas wish for her son, Stone tells us how this came about after her death. He states:

"Mrs. Stone, in getting out our Christmas ornaments, ran across many of the lovely Christmas cards we had saved, including a Christmas Card from Mother. My wife's thoughtfulness in placing the card at my breakfast plate brought me much happiness. Perhaps you can give this joy to a dear one, too."

—W. Clement Stone

This special gesture reminds one of the time Stone placed the $10.00 birthday gift underneath his mother's plate. Goodness has a way of showing up again and again, and this little miracle of a Christmas Card from Mother started with Stone's gesture of the unexpected birthday gift. As the saying goes, "What goes around comes around."

How to Develop the Habit of Enthusiasm
by Napoleon Hill

You can develop the habit of controlled enthusiasm by taking the following steps:
- Adopt a definite major purpose.
- Write out a clear statement of both your definite major purpose and the plan by which you hope to attain it. Include a statement of what you intend to give in return for its realization.
- Back your purpose with an enthusiastic motive and let that motive become a burning (obsessional) desire. Fan it, coax it, and let it become a dominating factor in your mind at all times.
- Go to work immediately to carry out your plan, starting right where you are.

- Follow your plan accurately and with persistence, fed by all the enthusiasm you can generate.
- If you are overtaken by temporary defeat, study your plans carefully and change them if necessary, but do not change your major purpose simply because you have met with a temporary setback.
- If the nature of your definite major purpose requires it, ally yourself with others whose aid you require, following the instructions given in the lesson on the master mind.
- Keep far away from joy-killers and pessimists and associate with those who are optimistic. Tell your plans to those who are in sympathy with you, such as members of your master mind alliance.
- Never let a day pass without devoting some time, though it be ever so little, to furthering your plans. Remember, you are developing the habit of enthusiasm, and habits call for repetition through physical action.
- Autosuggestion is a powerful factor in the development of the habit of enthusiasm, as well as in the development of any other habit. Therefore, keep yourself sold on the belief that you will obtain the object of your definite major purpose, no matter how far removed from you it may be. Your own mental attitude will determine the nature of the action your subconscious mind will take in connection with the fulfillment of your purpose.
- Keep your mind positive at all times. Enthusiasm will not mix with fear, envy, greed, jealousy, doubt, revenge, hatred, intolerance and procrastination. Enthusiasm thrives only on positive thought and action.

Your job will never be any bigger than your imagination makes it.

Remember, every person lives in two worlds: the world of his own mental attitude, which is greatly influenced by his associates and his surroundings, and the physical world in which he must struggle for a living. The physical world in which you make a living may be beyond your control, but you can, to a great extent, shape the circumstances of your immediate physical world. It can be done by the way you relate yourself to your mental world, for your mental attitude attracts to you those aspects of the physical world which harmonize with your mental attitude. Thus, pessimism will attract misery and ill fortune. But enthusiasm, properly controlled, will attract happiness and good fortune.

Source: *PMA Science of Success Course*. Pgs. 248, 249, & 250.

GOOD ^{AS} GOLD
19

Each year, the Napoleon Hill World Learning Center offers an open house to familiarize area residents and students with Hill's philosophies. Among his 17 principles are definiteness of purpose, creative vision and enthusiasm.

–Sue Ellen Reed

As a consequence of hard work and dedication, Stone became the President of Combined Insurance Company of America, served as President of the Chicago Boys' Clubs, Editor and Publisher of *Success Unlimited* magazine, and Chairman of the Napoleon Hill Foundation. He is co-author with Napoleon Hill of *Success Through a Positive Mental Attitude* and co-author with Norma Lee Browning of *The Other Side of the Mind* and he is the sole author of the all-time classic self-help book *The Success System that Never Fails.*

Stone is best remembered for his famous self-motivators such as "What the mind can conceive and believe, the mind can achieve with PMA!" The classic catch phrase "Do it now!" is immediately able to energize a person with just three simple words. Finally, to begin the day on the right note Stone encourages everyone to say and repeat with enthusiasm, "I feel healthy! I feel happy! I feel terrific!" Why use these self-motivators? Stone states: "Thinking good thoughts, positive and cheerful thoughts, will improve the way you feel. What affects your mind also affects your body."

In summary, Stone states:

The true value of a self-help book is not what the writer puts into the book, but what you, the reader, take out of the book and put into your life.

And,

You are the product of your heredity, environment, physical body, conscious and subconscious mind, experience, and particular position and direction in time and space . . . and something more, including powers known and unknown. You have the power to affect, use, control, or harmonize with all of them. And you can direct your thoughts, control your emotions and ordain your destiny.

Until his death at age 100, Stone remained the Chairman of the Napoleon Hill Foundation and worked diligently to disseminate the Success Principles that are listed below. His legacy continues at both Purdue University Calumet, Hammond, Indiana and at the University of Virginia's College at Wise. Both Don Green and Judith Williamson share in the mission of educating individuals regarding these principles through publications, seminars, workshops, retreats, and talks that instruct interested individuals and companies in the teachings of both Dr. Napoleon Hill and W. Clement Stone.

Success Principles according to W. Clement Stone
1. A Positive Mental Attitude
2. Definiteness of Purpose
3. Going the Extra Mile
4. Accurate Thinking
5. Self-Discipline
6. The Master Mind Alliance
7. Applied Faith
8. A Pleasing Personality
9. Personal Initiative
10. Enthusiasm
11. Controlled Attention

12. Teamwork
13. Learning from Adversity and Defeat
14. Creative Vision
15. Budgeting Time and Money
16. Maintaining Sound Physical and Mental Health
17. Using Cosmic Habit Force (Universal Law)

How to Get into the Two Percent Class of People Who Become Successful
by Napoleon Hill

Here are some suggestions of vital importance to you who sincerely desire to assimilate this philosophy of success and apply it to the achievement of the things you desire most in life:

- Adjust yourself to other people's states of mind and their peculiarities so that you can get along peacefully with them. Observe a dog and learn the art of self-control by watching how quickly he adjusts himself to the moods of his master.
- Refrain from taking notice of trivial circumstances in your human relations by refusing to allow them to become controversial incidents. Big people always avoid small incidents in human relations by ignoring them completely.
- Establish your own technique for conditioning your mind at the start of each day, based upon the instructions presented in this course, so you can maintain a positive mental attitude throughout the day.
- Learn the art of selling yourself to others by indirection rather than by direct approach.
- Adopt the habit of having a hearty laugh as a means of transmuting anger into a harmless emotion, and observe how effectively this will change your mind from negative to positive. Master salesmen follow this habit daily as a means of conditioning their own minds

with a positive mental attitude. This is particularly essential in the work of selling.

- Analyze your adversities, failures and defeats and determine the causes for them. Then observe how quickly you will discover the seed of an equivalent benefit which comes with such experiences.
- Concentrate your mind on the can do portion of tasks you undertake and do not worry about the cannot do portion unless and until it meets you face to face. By that time the can do portion will probably have already brought you very close to success.
- Learn to transmute all unpleasant circumstances into action which calls for a positive mental attitude. Make this a habit and follow this habit after every unpleasant experience.
- Recognize that every circumstance which influences your life to any extent is usable grist for your mill of life, and make it pay off in some form of benefit, whether the circumstance is pleasant or unpleasant.
- Recognize that no one can win all of the time no matter how much he may deserve to win. Learn to make allowances for the times when you will not win by transmuting the loss into some sort of gain from your experiences.
- Learn to look upon life as a continuous process of learning from experiences, both the good and the bad.
- Remember every thought you release comes back greatly multiplied, to bless or curse you. Watch your thought releases and make sure you send out only those whose fruits you are willing to receive in return.
- Be careful of your associates because the negative mental attitude of other people is very contagious and it rubs off on one a little at a time.
- Remember that you have a dual personality: one is positive and has a great capacity for belief; the other is negative and has an equally great capacity for disbelief. Place yourself on the side of the personality which believes and the other personality will

disappear because of lack of exercise.

- Remember that prayer brings the best results when the one who is praying has sufficient faith to see himself already in possession of that for which he prays. This calls for a positive mental attitude.

Source: *PMA Science of Success.* Pgs. 233, 234, & 235.

GOOD AS GOLD
20

True success is not achieved by those in fear of failing. Success–however you define it–is available only to those with Definiteness of Purpose supported with unrelenting action plans, a willingness to take risks, the ability to learn from mistakes and an unwavering belief that the power to achieve one's goal is founded in knowing that you are both worthy and capable of achieving it.

–Gail Brooks

Recently, Chino Martinez and I had the privilege of presenting a session at the American Society for Quality's International Convention in Minneapolis, Minnesota. If you are familiar with this organization, you are already aware of their international status and stellar reputation. Since many of the offerings center around quality in management coupled with accuracy in measurement, it is a difficult task to propose a presentation that ASQ would consider as an appropriate offering to their membership. However, for the second time our proposal was selected and our session entitled "Transforming Quality from Within with the Classics" was presented on Tuesday, May 19, 2009. The talk involved examining *The Wizard of Oz* and correlating the characteristics of the Lion, Tin Man, Scarecrow, and Dorothy with principles from Dr. Hill's success philosophy.

Since many of our readers are familiar with this classic children's story, I thought that you would enjoy and benefit from an overview of the talk. It will be presented in three parts over the next three weeks.

Transforming Quality from Within with the Classics

Children often use fairy tales to work through developmental stages that are causing emotional, mental, social, spiritual and physical growing pains in their young lives. It is easier to ask a question or raise a concern about a Lion, a Scarecrow, a Tin Man, or a Dorothy than it is to admit that the question is personal. Employees and management often prefer to address work related issues by using allegorical stories too instead of real life scenarios. For most people, it is preferential to discuss things in the abstract rather than the concrete. The classic tale, *The Wizard of Oz*, deals with confronting issues and fears that children need to overcome to mature. It also sets the stage for addressing what traits people need in the adult world to succeed if they are to grow and find their own personal strength and potential. Being naïve, cowardly, stupid, and heartless, are characteristics that can afflict anyone during certain periods in life, so it is easy to relate to L. Frank Baum's storybook characters.

In life and literature, personal growth and change are necessities for character advancement. Knowing personal shortcomings is fifty percent of the solution, but the essential part that allows someone to make the transition is equally critical. Knowledge is insufficient, courage is insufficient, and caring is insufficient. Combined, however, these ingredients are what comprise true leadership traits for the 21st century. "People do not care how much you know until they know how much you care," is an often repeated maxim. Until a person undergoes a transformation like the Cowardly Lion, the Scarecrow, and the Tin Man, no amount of leadership training will magically change a follower into a charismatic leader for the 21st century. Only a change of heart, mind, and soul will do that.

In anticipating the process a person must undergo in order to change into a leader, Napoleon Hill questioned what attributes a leader must possess. In his twenty years of research, Dr. Hill concluded that there are 17 Principles, or traits, that leaders must utilize. As Dorothy journeys to find her "rainbow," she discovers that the road to success is universal in application. Let's consider what principles she finds useful along her path.

Make success a habit. Horace Mann said, "Habit is a cable; we weave a thread of it every day, and at last we cannot break it." Nature maintains the entire universe through the system of established habits that never vary. For individuals, thoughts create our habits. Each of us is a composite result of the thoughts we have had to date. "You are where you are and what you are because of your established habits of thought and deed," states Dr. Napoleon Hill. If you wish to be something other than you are, cultivate the kinds of success habits that will take you from where you are to where you want to be. Just as Dorothy discovered that the key to her heart's desire–to return home–was always inside her, she still had to discover how to release her potential.

See if you can imagine what success principles will be useful to Dorothy and her team as she journeys down the yellow brick road to meet the Wizard.

The Voluntary Establishment of a Habit
by Napoleon Hill

There are only three principles underlying the voluntary establishment of a habit. They are very important, so remember them well:

a. **Plasticity**, which is simply the property or capability of changing or being changed. It also implies that once a change has been made, the new form established remains until a subsequent change modifies it. In other words, plasticity is the sort of flexibility found in a piece of modeling clay used by children in school. It may be molded into any desired shape and it will remain in that shape until it is molded into a different shape. Man, of all living creatures, is the only one who possesses this characteristic of being plastic, of being capable of change, and his plasticity lies, of course, in his mental faculties. Man may be changed by external influences or his environment; or he may voluntarily change himself, by exercise of his will power. This prerogative obviously is a basic necessity for the formation of voluntary habits.

b. **Frequency of Impression**. As we have seen, repetition is the mother of memory. It is also the mother of habits. One of the factors affecting the speed with which a habit can be established is how often the action or thought involved is repeated. This, of course, varies with the individual, the circumstances, and the element of time. A thought can be repeated only so many times a day, for instance, and if a man is at work, circumstances may prevent his thinking of the particular habit he wishes to establish. There is also the matter of personal initiative. A man may be lazy and indifferent, or he may be ambitious and energetic. This will affect the number of times he will repeat the action or thought. This, in turn, affects the length of time it will take him to establish the habit.

c. **Intensity of Impression**. Here is another variable in the process of establishing a habit pattern. All through these principles you have been told of the importance of a strong, compelling motive, and a burning desire, as essentials. Here is the reason. If an idea is impressed upon the mind, backed with all the emotion you are capable of, it will become an obsessional desire. Thus it will have a greater impact than if you simply express an idle wish, even though the words you employ are identical. The degree of intensity of impression is, therefore, another factor which affects the speed with which a habit may be developed and set.

Source: *PMA Science of Success* Course. Pgs. 505 & 506.

GOOD ^{AS} GOLD
21

My most valuable self-education lessons began with reading two classics: **The Master Key to Riches** *and* **Think and Grow Rich** *by Napoleon Hill. These books made me long for better and deeper associations with successful people and to seek the abundant wisdom of other great leaders and thinkers.*

–Chuck Sink

Even though the ruby red slippers were on her feet, she needed concrete directions as to how to make them work their magic. Likewise, personal knowledge, compassion, and courage are worthy human attributes that are acquired in proportion to their giving. Dorothy needed to acquire these traits in order to mature. Her wanderings in Oz caused her to reflect and to grow proportionate to her experiences.

American philosopher, Ralph Waldo Emerson states, "The key to every man is his thought." Napoleon Hill adds that, "In this manner you may control your earthly destiny to an astounding degree—simply by exercising your privilege of shaping your own thoughts, but once these thoughts have been shaped into definite patterns, they are taken over by the law of cosmic habitforce and are made into permanent habits—and they remain as such unless and until they are supplanted by different and stronger thought patterns."

In order to become a leader in your chosen field, you must possess the traits of a leader. These traits are: Knowledge, Courage, and Compassion. By looking more closely at the Scarecrow, the Cowardly Lion, and the Tin Man, one can begin to understand what these characteristics mean to today's leaders.

Knowledge is essential in any field of endeavor, but simply having the textbook how-to is insufficient when it comes to leading the field. Perhaps you know of people who have made the same assumption the Scarecrow made in believing that Knowledge is Power. More accurately, knowledge is only potential power. It is only power when you use it. Knowledge is only one stage in the six-step process of the larger idea of learning. True learning, according to Bloom, occurs in these stages: knowledge, comprehension, application, analysis, synthesis, and evaluation. Notice that knowledge is at the bottom, not at the top of the hierarchy. Knowledge about industry, people, technology, products, business, and anything else is relatively useless until you apply it.

As the Scarecrow advanced in his learning, he qualified for his diploma. Ask yourself, was he really any smarter after he got his diploma or did he just think he was? Once he acquired the knowledge, his self-esteem was enhanced, and he had more confidence which in turn allowed him to apply his knowledge. Applied knowledge is power. Now instead of thinking in terms of self-imposed limitations, the Scarecrow thinks in terms of ability and outcome. His thoughts become his reality. Definiteness of Purpose is the starting point of all achievement. This one principle separates the "doers" from the "drifters" in life.

Courage is the ability to take out the garbage even when the porch light is not lit. It is confronting fear in the face and having the nerve to proceed regardless of the outcome. Napoleon Hill states that "Fear is the greatest obstacle to success." It can stop a person dead in his tracks. It causes a person to look back and not ahead. Franklin D. Roosevelt's powerful statement "We have nothing to fear but fear itself," is as true today as when he uttered it decades ago during the Great Depression in the United States. Fear immobilizes us. It makes us followers instead of leaders. It depletes our personal initiative and enthusiasm. Essentially, it diminishes our drive and desire to succeed. When the Cowardly Lion is awarded his medal for courage, he still felt the fear but understood that even courageous people feel fear. He thought that he was courageous and consequently he became so. The medal became an outward validation for an inner change. Once fear is analyzed for what it is, an individual must look to the desired outcome and decide whether moving through his fear into action is what he wants to do. By not becoming intimidated by overwhelming amounts of information, people, or any of the other major fears, individuals can embrace their fears and advance in life if the perceived payoff is worth this change. Dr. Hill states that "The person seeking success must force himself to control his fear by taking the first step toward his goal."

In death and dying research, Dr. Elizabeth Kubler Ross states that there are five stages that individuals experience in the dying process. The stages are: denial, anger, bargaining, depression, and acceptance. People intent on confronting a fear move through these very same stages since these stages mirror the change process. Knowing that there is a sequence of steps that people need to take in order to change makes the process more rational and controllable for individuals. Positive Mental Attitude enables each of us to retain the "I can" attitude even in the face of fear. It is the right mental attitude in all circumstances.

Two Important Laws
by Napoleon Hill

There are two important laws with which you should become familiar. One is the law of compensation and the other is the law of increasing returns. Mankind is dependent upon the operation of these two laws for its very life. If the farmer did not comply with them he could produce no food. Let us see how he must necessarily observe these laws plus the principle of going the extra mile, whether he consciously recognizes it or not.

The farmer must clear the soil of trees and shrubs. Then he must plow, harrow and fertilize where necessary. After this he must put seed in the soil. He must mix intelligence with his labor, observing the proper season of the year for planting, the correct method of crop culture, and the right irrigation and cultivation techniques.

With these steps completed, he has done all he can do. Up to this point he has not been paid for his labor. He has literally done more than he has been paid for! Now he must wait for nature to germinate the seed and for time to elapse, during which growth occurs and a crop is produced.

If the farmer has performed his labor intelligently, nature will reward him through the law of compensation, by which she neither permits any living thing to get something for nothing, nor allows any form of labor to go unrewarded. This law assures the return of the seed which was planted. But with a return of the seed alone, nothing would have been gained by the process, and no food could be produced for man or beast.

There must be another law operating at the same time. It is the law of increasing returns, for there is an increase in the amount produced over the amount planted. Nature gives back to the farmer the seed he planted in the ground plus a margin of many times the amount of seed. This is his reward for having done more than he was temporarily paid for. This unvarying law always rewards intelligent effort rendered in the attitude of faith, and rendered unstintingly without regard to the limits of immediate compensation.

Now you can understand the statement that this strategic principle of rendering more and better service than one is presently paid for is not a man-made law. Of course, you may think that these examples are simple. They are simple enough so far as effects are concerned, but you would hardly consider the cause behind them as simple. That cause is as profound and imponderable as the other laws by which this planet and the entire universe are maintained in an orderly and harmonious manner throughout time and space.

Nature has definite, established laws and principles to which man must adapt himself if he wishes to live successfully. It is not necessary for us to grasp the broad meaning and purpose of these laws. All we need do is observe their existence and adapt our actions to them.

Source: *PMA Science of Success Course*. Pgs. 142 & 143.

GOOD _{AS} GOLD
22

We must give ourselves the power to take control of our thoughts, to overcome our fears and follow our Yellow Brick Road of rules to accomplish our dreams and goals. No one can do it for us. Because: THE REAL WIZARD OF OZ IS IN YOU! And don't let anyone take that truth from you.

–Barbara Hailey

Compassion–The Tin Man:

You cannot expect to become an empowered leader without just and fair attitudes toward others. Compassion, leading by the heart, is not a characteristic that is acquired at birth but one that is gained through human interaction. In *A Christmas Carol*, the Ghost of Christmas Yet to Come calls compassion the milk of human kindness. Caring begins with the relationship a child has with its mother, grows to people within the family, and then outward to the community and beyond. In Maslow's Hierarchy of Needs, it is shown that in order for a person to return the gifts that he has been given at birth, he needs to be first cared for himself. Without a compassionate model to follow, the student does not acquire compassion. Compassion requires an interest in giving, not getting. It means Going the Extra Mile for the purpose of giving back to the Universe because of the gifts that were provided to you at birth. Maslow shows one of the higher order needs as self-actualization. This is the stage wherein a person is able to return to the Universe the gifts that he has been given through the use of his talents. When the Tin Man is recognized for having a heart, he emotionally feels his interconnectedness to others. He experiences emotional pain and hurt as he knows in his heart that Dorothy is returning to Kansas. This higher order need of compassion is what makes us human.

Napoleon Hill tells us that we should pattern our relations with others on the rules of conduct given in the Sermon on the Mount. He goes on to add that without spiritual success material achievements are a mockery. Hill's warning: "Remember: the brand of justice you mete out to others will be judged by your own conscience." He adds, "The sort of justice I mean is positive—aimed at inspiring others to greater productiveness through recognition of their worth and capabilities as human beings." Going the Extra Mile is the GEM of all principles. It causes the Universe to reward us in compound interest upon compound interest. This is known as the Law of Increasing Returns and is put into motion by the Law of Compensation. Store up this type of wealth for yourself, and you will never question your accomplishments in life.

Conclusions–The Wizard of Oz–A Roadmap to the 21st Century

After comparing the characters in The Wizard of Oz with yourself as you journey through life, it can be seen that within each of us is a Cowardly Lion, a Tin Man, a Scarecrow, and a Dorothy. These "characters" are learning opportunities that each of us has been given to enhance our earthly performance. More importantly, if we aspire toward organizational leadership, we must embrace these learning opportunities and accept the challenges that they provide in order to mature within our profession. By stepping forward and embracing the challenge, we can walk through the challenge and not be hindered or frightened by the opportunity growth provides. Shakespeare states: "There is a tide in the affairs of men which, taken at the flood, leads on to fortune. Omitted, all the voyage of their life is bound in shallows and in miseries." He cautions, "Time and tide wait for no man." Accept the challenge life provides. Seize the opportunity and make that change. It's good for you. Just ask Dorothy, the Tin Man, the Cowardly Lion, and the Scarecrow. Each received their just reward, and life for them became better because of the learning that they encountered along the yellow brick road.

Conceive, Believe, and Achieve--life's "ABC's" of success only in reverse. Take it one step at a time. Just follow your yellow brick road and you will arrive at your destination sooner than you think. And, you won't be in Kansas anymore!

Everyone Can Perform "Miracles"
by Napoleon Hill

A positive mental attitude is the habit of keeping the mind busily engaged in connection with the circumstances and things one desires in life, and off the things one does not desire. The majority of people go all the way through life with their mental attitudes dominated by fears and anxieties and worries over circumstances which somehow have a way of making their appearance sooner or later. And the strange part of this truth is that these people often blame other people for the misfortunes they have thus brought upon themselves by their negative mental attitudes.

The mind has a definite way of clothing one's thoughts in appropriate physical equivalents. Think in terms of poverty and you will live in poverty. Think in terms of opulence and you will attract opulence. Through the eternal law of harmonious attraction one's thoughts always clothe themselves in material things appropriate unto their nature.

A positive mental attitude is the habit of looking upon all unpleasant circumstances with which one meets as merely opportunities for one to test his capacity to rise above them by searching for the "seed of an equivalent benefit" and putting it to work.

A positive mental attitude is the habit of evaluating all

problems, and distinguishing the difference between those one can master and those one cannot control. The person with a positive mental attitude endeavors to solve the problems he can control, and so relates himself to those he cannot control that they do not influence his mental attitude from positive to negative.

Source: *You Can Work Your Own Miracles.*
Napoleon Hill. Ballantine Book. 1971. Pg. 21.

GOOD AS GOLD
23

Negative outcomes are produced by negative thoughts which are the product of negative conversations. Perceived bad outcomes are produced by the bad news that we have chosen to dwell on.

–Keith Russell Lee

"No bad news" is the partial refrain from a song from *The Wiz*. When "bad news" prevails it can gain momentum and ruin our day and even our lives if we allow it. It can cast a very real spell that cannot only harm us but hinder our joy and advancement for years to come. Literally, bad news can suck our soul out of us and make us feel as if we are already dead–a zombie who sleepwalks through life. The only antidote for bad news is its replacement with positive thoughts. Both Dr. Hill and W. Clement Stone remind us to look bad news in its evil eye, turn it on its heel, and send it packing. But, as anyone knows who has experienced a setback, a shocking loss, a hardship, or just a negative emotion, making a change can be literally as difficult as turning the tide. How can we turn the tide when it seems beyond our doing?

I am reminded of a quote by Edmund Burke that states: "All that is necessary for the triumph of evil is that good men do nothing." Napoleon Hill adds: "Learn to motivate others by example." It seems that the cure is in the doing, in the action steps that can be taken to not only place your finger in the hole in the wall to contain the tide, but to take steps to sandbag the shore, build a retaining wall, and then attend to the real problem that is causing the flooding. It's

111

not one step, but many, and the final difference will be that the entire village is not washed away. You can be a part of the change that you want to see in the world, just as Gandhi states. It only requires positive action on your part.

With the passing of Michael Jackson, the world had "no good news." In my classes I often use his music video "Man in the Mirror" as an illustration of how we can be the change we want to see in the world. The images of starving children, the homeless, warfare, and nuclear weapons are difficult to view, but these very images are able to stir up indignation in our souls for allowing it to happen on our watch. This video forces us out of our comfort zone, our zombie day-to-day existence, and sends us a battle cry for reform. It is "no good news," but the alternative–change–can be. For this positive message in a negative world, I thank Michael Jackson for bringing it to our attention. A gifted work always lives beyond the life of the artist who created it, and this video will inspire us to action for the time it takes for the world to clean up its act. With Michael in a higher position now, I am sure that he will continue to assist in the work he began on this planet. We are better for his having been here, but his work is not done. We are the hands and feet that need to do the work of making the world a better place in which to live! In Michael's words: "Make that change!"

What Steps Can You Take To Develop A Positive Mental Attitude?
by Napoleon Hill

A positive mental attitude is a 'must' for all who wish to make life pay off on their own terms. Nothing great was ever achieved without a positive mental attitude.

Recognize that your mental attitude is the one and only thing over which you, and you alone, have complete control, and exercise the privilege of taking possession of and directing your mind with a positive mental attitude.

Realize, and prove to your own satisfaction, that every

adversity, failure, defeat, sorrow and unpleasant circumstance, whether of your own making or otherwise, carries with it the seed of an equivalent benefit which may be transmuted into a blessing of great proportions.

Learn to close the door of your mind on all the failures and unpleasant circumstances of the past, and clear your mind so that it can operate in a positive mental attitude.

Find out what you want most in life and begin getting it, right where you now stand, by helping others to acquire similar benefits, thus putting into action that magic success principle: the habit of going the extra mile.

Select the person who, in your opinion, is the finest person in all the world, past or present, and make that person your pacemaker for the remainder of your life, emulating him or her in every possible way.

Determine how great a supply of material riches you require, set up a plan for acquiring it, and then adopt the principle of not too much, not too little by which to govern your future ambition for material things. Greed for an over-abundance of material things has destroyed more people than any other cause.

Form the habit of saying or doing something every day which will make another person, or persons feel better. You can do this by a phone call, a kind word in passing, dropping a postal card, or by doing some other kindness for another. A good inspirational book placed in the hand of one who needs it could, for example, work wonders in the life of that person.

Source: *PMA Science of Success.* Pg. 225.

Napoleon Hill

GOOD AS GOLD
24

Freedom is a wonderful concept which we all desire. Those of us who live in the United States have much freedom which we accept without a great deal of thought. However, when we achieve real "freedom" it can often become a fearful responsibility.

–Dr. Judith Arcy

In the United States the month of July is dedicated to celebrations. On July 4th we celebrate the birth of our country. In keeping with tradition, we often celebrate with vacations, time off from work, family reunions, picnics and barbecues. Something special is always going on and an atmosphere of happy anticipation generally sets the tone for the entire month. Unlike other seasonal holidays, this summer one is not associated with the stress that can accompany the others. Being footloose and fancy free is the norm, and less becomes more. Fireworks, the sandy beach, hamburgers and hotdogs on the grill, and warm summer evenings all contribute to a carefree attitude that causes a person to slow down rather than speed up.

It is good to notice things that may seem insignificant at other times of the year. Things like the smell of newly mown grass, starlight and moonlight, the flashing light of fireflies, summer breezes, and the scent of flower and vegetable gardens. Although we may attribute these signposts of summer to the cycle of the seasons, the other reality is that we are reaping what we have sown.

In speaking of service, Dr. Hill reminds us to "Take a

lesson from the farmer who plows his ground, fertilizes it, plants the seed and then waits for the reaction which is sure to provide him with a rich harvest." Another familiar adage reminds us that we reap what we sow. If we plant tomatoes, then we can expect a harvest of tomatoes in due course–not ears of corn. The lesson is simple. If we follow the laws of nature, we know that we will be compensated for what we have done because the law of increasing returns will work in our favor. Our time of harvest will come and so will our rejoicing. We grow strong through work (service), and our compensation will happen sooner or later because it is a law. The longer we wait, the better it is for us because we will be compounding interest from the Universe!

So, on this July 4th, be grateful for the little gifts that are freely given to us by the Universe. A friend sent me an email that listed several ordinary miracles: a fresh pot of coffee you didn't make yourself...an unexpected phone call from an old friend...green stoplights on your way to work...the fastest line at the grocery store...a good sing-along song on the radio...your keys found right where you left them.

Why not create a list of your small miracles right now? Don't forget to add the freedom we enjoy in this country too as we celebrate our July 4th heritage!

Conceive, Believe, & Achieve
by Napoleon Hill

Whatever the mind of man conceives, man can achieve, so long as his conception does not run counter to any natural laws and is in harmony with a moral and orderly universe.

One of the purposes of man's existence here on earth seems to be to act as the receiver and distributor of the power of Infinite Intelligence. We can see that, to the extent that man cooperates in this purpose, he allies himself with the forces behind all nature. And, conversely, to the extent that he looks out only for his own selfish ends, he is opposing this power, or retarding its flow.

The power of Infinite Intelligence pours life into us as a flowing stream, maintaining all of the functions of our bodies and minds. We can use it to guide and govern the circumstances and conditions of our lives, if we act as conductors of this energy, and shape it according to our constructive purposes.

The inflowing power has no limitations. It is forced to manifest itself in this world in a way in which we, as individuals, can understand and express it.

Life energy flows into a positive, receptive mind in a continual stream, just as strips of aluminum alloy are fed into the punch presses of a fabricating plant. Going into it is potential life, potential abundance, potential power, potential riches. But, like the forced aluminum strips, our thoughts coming out can be only what we have expressed–what the stamping machines of our own convictions and beliefs have impressed upon the original material.

Whatever we accept, whatever we love, cherish or desire with a burning desire and hold constantly in our thoughts as our own, finds fulfillment in our lives. As sunlight, passing through a prism, is broken up into its component color rays, so Infinite Intelligence, in passing through our conscious mind, takes on a variety of forms. The prism of our minds can be darkened only by the imperfections of our own creations of worry, fear and failure consciousness, which shut out all the lighter, happier colors. It is a stream of intelligence that starts through us, but just as a poorly made die in the punch press can cut rude and ugly pieces from the best of raw material, just as a faulty prism can turn beams of sunshine into shadows, so can our disbeliefs and doubts turn perfect life-energy into sickness, poverty, discord and misery.

The first essential then, is to be careful of the pattern of the die, to watch your desires and beliefs as carefully as the director of the United States Mint watches the die that casts the silver coins. Instead of picturing the things you fear and do not want, and thus stamping a negative on the Infinite Intelligence flowing into your mind, be sure to picture the conditions you do want.

If you would have faith, keep your mind on that which you want and off that which you do not want.

Source: *PMA Science of Success Course.* Pgs. 88 & 89.

GOOD ^{AS} GOLD
25

If the thing you wish to do is right, and you believe in it with a burning desire, don't let anything stop you from doing it.

–Phil Barlow

Dr. Hill states: "There can be no fixed price on the value of organized thinking! But there is no power in thought until it is organized and directed toward a definite end and implemented by intelligent action." If there is one underlying key to success in the Science of Success it is thought followed by intelligent action. Thought without action or action without thought will never deliver life's riches to a person. Thought + Action must be the combination that equals the desired result in one's personal quest.

In teaching this concept, I often refer to the poem by Edgar Allan Poe entitled *Eldorado*. It reads:

Gaily bedight,
A gallant knight,
In sunshine and in shadow,
Had journeyed long,
Singing a song,
In search of Eldorado.

But he grew old—
This knight so bold—
And o'er his heart a shadow
Fell, as he found
No spot of ground
That looked like Eldorado.

And, as his strength
Failed him at length,
He met a pilgrim shadow—
"Shadow," said he,
"Where can it be—
This land of Eldorado?"

"Over the Mountains
Of the Moon,
Down the Valley of the Shadow,
Ride, boldly ride,"
The shade replied,
"If you seek for Eldorado!"

At first reading the message in this poem is not so obvious. A knight setting out on a gallant quest for Eldorado–the golden land–seems to be following the right path. Later, it appears as time passes and his reserve falters, that perhaps his personal GPS is inaccurate. Was the data provided incomplete, did his King give the wrong coordinates, or was the Knight just starry-eyed, dim-witted, or both? Perhaps, it is a combination of all of these things. But the real flaw in the program exists because the Knight's internal compass was not aligned with his North Star and he did not utilize accurate thinking. The initial thought was present. The action was present. But, the action did not emanate from intelligent thought that was combined with a definite major purpose. So when the Shadow shows up, the Knight is given more directions but these are even more elusive than he followed before. Perhaps the Shadow may represent the shadow of the Knight's former self as he despairs that his journey may never reach its destination. How could it reach a destination since he never knew where he was going, so how would he know when he got there?

Consider how you might be like the Knight in your quest for riches. Have you thoroughly examined the terrain before you set out on your quest? Do you really know what it is you are looking for? Are your directions and plan specific, organized, detailed, and spread out over a period of time with a reasonable deadline? Can you measure your progress by signposts along the way? As you progress, are you finding more of yourself or losing more of yourself in the journey? In Hill's article below, the twelve riches of life are outlined. If these are life's ultimate treasures, is your personal path leading toward them or away from them?

As Dr. Hill states: "Hopeful wishing a good starter, but a poor finisher." Before you begin your life's journey make absolutely certain that you have a treasure map worth following. You are the best judge on that account.

The Source of All Riches
by Napoleon Hill

Thought is the source of all riches, whether material, physical or spiritual. It is the means by which the twelve riches of life (*a positive mental attitude, sound physical health, harmony in human relationships, freedom from fear, the hope of achievement, the capacity for faith, willingness to share one's blessings, a labor of love, an open mind on all subjects, self-discipline, the capacity to understand people, and financial security*) may be appropriated by all who desire them. Yet thought is of little use in the accumulation of riches until it is organized and directed toward definite ends through definiteness of purpose. Like electricity, thought is a power which can, and often does, destroy as readily as it constructs, if it is not controlled and applied to constructive ends. Electricity will turn the wheels of industry, and convert darkness into light. Or it will snuff out life, according to the intelligence with which it is applied.

Thought will do the same, although it works in a different manner, through the brain of man. The pages of medical history are filled with the records of cases of people who have committed suicide through the negative application of thought. Every psychologist knows that the negative application of thought is responsible for much of the misery and poverty in the world. The world came into an understanding of the principle and usage of electricity very slowly, but it did learn at long last how to harness and use electricity. Slowly the world is learning how to harness and use the power of thought.

Men search throughout their lifetimes for worldly riches, not recognizing that the source of all riches is already within their reach and under their control, awaiting only its recognition and use. This is no mere assumption of truth, but it is a fact known to everyone who has become aware of the power of his own thought, and has appropriated that power and used it for the solution of his problems. For example, most men go all the way through life without recognizing the source of power which is available to them through the application of the master mind principle.

The accurate thinker not only recognizes the existence of this principle, but he makes use of it as a means of multiplying his own mind power. The accurate thinker surrounds himself with a master mind group consisting of at least four different types of talent: a spiritual adviser, a financial adviser, a health adviser and a personal adviser. Beyond this, you may require additional types of master mind allies, including technical advisers, professional advisers and other types of counselors, depending upon the nature and scope of your definite major purpose.

Source: *PMA Science of Success Course.* Pgs. 316 & 317.

GOOD ᴬˢ GOLD
26

The teachings and writings of Napoleon Hill are timeless. They apply as well today as they did in 1937 when **Think & Grow Rich** *was published. I commend them to you.*

–Richard Banta

Asking the question "How can I make the best of what I have?" can lead us in new, positive directions. Striving for perfection often puts us in a bad mood and can predispose us to certain failures in many areas of our life. If we fail to get started because the "perfect" outcome we envision is daunting, we never achieve what we are capable of doing. Instead of envisioning the picture perfect outcome for trivial things life hands us, why not just seek improvement rather than perfection?

For example, in cleaning your home you have probably heard the phrase that a "lick and a promise" will have to do. At certain times, this may be enough–granted that it is an improvement over what is. In preparing meals, home cooked ones can be the healthiest, but store bought ones can meet the need too if we are making healthy selections. In caring for our animals, daily grooming over a visit to the Kitty Spa or Puppy Palace may just have to do when funds are low. In automobile care, simply having a garbage bag available to collect refuse is a good idea to cut down on the clutter that can accumulate. All of these ideas are no more than common sense, but do we apply and use them? Probably not, because many of us fail to consider the continuum of actions that lead to success and instead focus on the 0% end or the 100% end. This stalls us in our tracks! Like a train without fuel, we become a person without enthusiasm because we cannot see an escalating scale toward a positive end result. How can we train ourselves to go toward the goal, but not lose sight of the steps in the journey? Perhaps it is as easy as answering the question that I began with–"How can I make the best of what I have?"

Attorney Richard Banta answers that question for you. Rather than throwing in the towel when a home based business did not meet his expectations, he took the best and left the rest. His focus on the open door of the future rather than the closed door of the past enabled him to take what he had learned from his initial attempt and apply it to a new business start. Isn't this a better approach than bemoaning that his first attempt wasn't perfect? I think so. Either we learn from our experiences or are defeated by them. The good news is that we can decide which it will be.

Begin simply. What tasks do you have before you today? Consider how you can tackle them and make an impact, but not worry about doing them perfectly. Perhaps you can wash the dishes, but let them air dry. Cut the grass but forego the trim. Wash the clothes but leave the ironing for later. The trick here is "a task begun is half done." Don't allow yourself to get stuck by waiting for the picture perfect outcome. The only way to achieve this positive end result is by taking one step at a time toward your goal. It doesn't have to happen in a day, week, or month, but it will never happen if you wait for the perfect opportunity to begin. Recognize that the perfect opportunity is now. And, the perfect outcome will only grace your doorstep when you have prepared the entryway for success.

Lessons Learned from Defeat
by Napoleon Hill

The most important moment in your life is when you recognize that you have met with defeat. It is the most important because it provides you with a dependable means to foretell the possibilities of your future success.

If you accept defeat as an inspiration to try again, with renewed confidence and determination, the attainment of your success will be only a matter of time. If you accept defeat as final and allow it to destroy your confidence, you may as well abandon your hope of success.

Every defeat you meet will mark an important turning point in your life, for defeat will bring you face to face with the necessity of renewing confidence in yourself, or of admitting that confidence is lacking.

Defeat often serves to relieve a man of his conceit. But there is a difference between conceit and self-reliance based upon an honest inventory of one's character. The man who quits when defeat overtakes him thereby indicates that he mistook his conceit for self-reliance.

If a man has genuine self-reliance, he also has sound character, for one springs from the other. And a sound character does not yield to defeat without a fight.

Education, skill and experience are useful assets in every calling, but they will be of little value to the man who, like the Arab of the desert, folds up his tent and silently steals away when he is defeated. The man with a definite major purpose, faith and determination may occasionally be swept from the success side of the River of Life by circumstances beyond his control, but he will not long remain there. For his mental reaction to his defeat will be sufficiently strong to carry him back to the success side where he rightfully belongs.

Failure and adversity have introduced many men to opportunities which they would not have recognized under more favorable circumstances.

A man's mental attitude in respect to defeat is the factor of major importance in determining whether he rides with the tides of fortune on the success side of the River of Life or is swept to the failure side of circumstances of misfortune.

The circumstances which separate failure from success often are so slight that their real cause is overlooked. Often they exist entirely in the mental attitude with which one meets temporary defeat. The man with a positive mental attitude reacts to defeat in a spirit of determination not to accept it. The man with a negative mental attitude reacts to defeat in a spirit of hopeless acceptance.

The man who maintains a positive mental attitude may have anything in life upon which he may set his heart, so long as it does not conflict with the laws of God and the rights of his fellowmen. He probably will experience many defeats, but he will not surrender to defeat. He will convert it into a stepping stone from which he will rise to higher and higher areas of achievement.

Source: *PMA Science of Success course*. Pgs. 394, 395 & 396.

GOOD ᴬˢ GOLD
27

*I find that when we calm our mind, we give a chance
for our subconscious mind to talk–which speaks to
us through our intuition.*

–Ray Stendall

Here are some quotations by Dr. Hill that can easily be turned into positive autosuggestions for your personal use. By repeating them daily or even several times a day, these statements can begin to create a pathway in your brain much like a groove in an old-fashioned record. Then, when it is time to call up a positive sense of well-being that will see you through in times of need, all you have to do is "replay" the suggestion. W. Clement Stone knew this when he always recited "I feel healthy, I feel happy, I feel terrific." And, his ever famous "Do it now!" puts us on the success track because of the call to action. Literally, Stone gives us our marching orders.

Still skeptical? Give it a try for a week or more, and see if you can condition your mind for a positive mental attitude. What have you got to lose? "Do the thing and you shall have the power," states Emerson. If you are success conscious, you will attract success just as easily as you will attract failure. Conceive, believe, achieve!

Below are my examples–you can use these or create your own.

Keep your mind on the things you want and off the things you don't want.

I keep my mind on the things I want and off the things I do not want.

Set your mind on a definite goal and observe how quickly the world stands aside to let you pass.
I have a definite goal and all doors open effortlessly before me.

All things are possible to the person who believes they are possible.
I know all things are possible.

The secret of getting things done is to act. The way to success is organized thinking followed by action! action! action!
I think first and then act.

Do it now . . . and before anyone tells you to do it!
I do it now.

You are the master of your destiny. You can influence, direct and control your own environment. You can make your life what you want it to be.
I control my destiny by controlling my thoughts and emotions. I act in accordance with my highest good.

Whine about your misfortunes and thereby multiply them, or keep still and starve them out.
I dwell on my successes.

Riches begin with thoughts.
My thoughts are my treasure.

That which you think today becomes that which you are tomorrow.
I think positively and create positive results now.

You are where you are because of your habits of thought.

My thoughts create my life.

Autosuggestion and Controlled Attention
by Napoleon Hill

You are influenced by, and you are a part of, the dominating circumstances of your daily environment. The medium by which this takes place is known as autosuggestion (suggestions you make to yourself, either consciously or unconsciously).

Autosuggestion records in your memory every thought you express, and makes it a part of your character, whether the thought is positive or negative. It records every word which is spoken within your hearing, and gives it a positive or a negative meaning, according to your reaction to it.

Autosuggestion records your thought reactions to everything you see or recognize through any of the five physical senses, and it records the "feel" which you pick up from your physical surroundings.

The objects on which you deliberately concentrate your attention become the dominating influences in your environment. If your thoughts are fixed upon poverty, or the physical signs of poverty, these influences are transferred to your subconscious mind through autosuggestion.

If the habit of concentrating on poverty is continued, it will result in conditioning your mind to accept poverty as an unavoidable circumstance, and you will eventually become poverty-conscious. This is how millions of people condemn themselves to a life of poverty. Remember this, you who would have opulence.

The principle of autosuggestion works in precisely the same manner when your dominating thoughts are fixed, through controlled attention upon opulence and economic security. This habit leads to the development of a prosperity consciousness without which no one may hope for economic security.

It is obvious, therefore, that when you voluntarily fix

your attention upon a definite major purpose of a positive nature, and force your mind, through daily habits of thought, to dwell on that subject, you condition your subconscious mind to act on that purpose. As we have stated repeatedly, the subconscious mind acts first on the dominating thoughts placed before it daily, whether they are positive or negative, and proceeds to carry out those thoughts by translating them into their material equivalent.

Source: *PMA Science of Success.* Pgs. 345 & 346.

GOOD ^AS^ GOLD
28

Whenever you start to feel listless and lacking passion, ask yourself, what gives my life meaning? The answer, more often than not, will tell you what you need to do to recapture enthusiasm.

–Mark Sanborn

Have you ever taken a photograph? Or, are you a photographer? Regardless of your credentials, I feel it is safe to say that the photographs you have taken that have turned out best were those captured when you took the time to focus. By fine tuning the lens, your subject ultimately became more in tune with the picture already in place in your mind's eye. As you worked to capture in a frame what you already envisioned on the screen of your mind, your photograph "developed" into reality. Interestingly enough, the realization of our long term and short term goals are really not so different than this picture taking technique.

The more we focus, the better the results we achieve. It takes controlled attention to focus on a regular basis. Once we master this technique the application of this principle leads to mastery in our chosen area. In order to do an excellent job we must focus only on the task while we are doing it–no matter if it is typing a letter, baking a cake, driving a car, painting a masterpiece or planting a garden. Focus involves actively aligning our cognitive abilities with our desired outcome.

Remember in school when your teacher loudly said "Pay attention!"? The point of that command is to relieve you from your daydreams and draw you back into the reality of the lesson. There is a time and place too for creative imagination, but not while you are working on succeeding in something non-related but ultimately important. By paying close attention to the task at hand, you are notifying your conscious mind that you are in charge. Otherwise, by being wishy-washy and unfocused, you are not the Captain of your ship. Your watch is left unmanned, and disaster could strike any minute.

Practice focusing in time increments. If you have a task that you are reluctant to complete, tell yourself that you will give it your utmost for 15, 30, or 60 minutes. You set the time you are comfortable with at first. Then, stay with the task for the chosen amount of time. As you become comfortable controlling the outcome and also begin to see positive results, you will understand that by focusing on your goal you stay at the wheel of your ship and guide yourself to your chosen destination.

So focus, focus, focus, and your life's journey will end up exactly at the destination you determined well in advance. Only you can make it so.

Controlled Attention Leads to Mastery
by Napoleon Hill

Controlled attention leads to mastery in any type of human endeavor, because it enables one to focus the powers of his mind upon the attainment of a definite objective and to keep it so fixed at will. Controlled attention is self-mastery of the highest order, for it is an accepted fact that the man who controls his own mind may control everything else that gets in his way.

It was this sort of control which Harriet Beecher Stowe had in mind when she said:

> *When you get into a tight place and everything goes against you, 'til it seems as though you could not hold on a minute longer, never give up then, for that is just the*

place and time that the tide will turn.

The tide seems always to turn in your favor if you are determined to see that it does. Your state of mind has everything to do with turning the tide. Plato expressed this thought in his statement:

The first and best victory is to conquer self; to be conquered by self is, of all things, the most shameful and vile.

Francis Parkman showed his understanding of the power of the mind, and particularly the power available through controlled attention, when he wrote:

He who would do some great thing in this short life must apply himself to work with such concentration of his forces as, to idle spectators, who live only to amuse themselves, looks like insanity.

Washington Irving expressed his respect for the power of the mind in these words:

Great minds have purposes, others have wishes. Little minds are tamed and subdued by misfortune; but great minds rise above them.

The potentialities of the power of controlled attention, through concentration, are many, but none of them is greater, nor more important, than that of concentration upon a definite major purpose. Hidden in these two words: controlled attention–is a strange power that will enable you to remove all self-imposed limitations which most people accept or set up in their own minds, and by which some are bound throughout their lives.

Source: *PMA Science of Success Course.* Pgs. 334 & 335.

GOOD AS GOLD
29

There is plenty of bad in the world and if you don't have a steady moral compass, you can be pulled in the direction of very destructive actions which will flood into your moral vacuum.

–Eliezer A. Alperstein

Why teach children about the penalties that life has to offer when you could just as easily teach them about the rewards? Fear based education is negative and faith based education is positive. Simply put, this means that whether we are fearful or faithful, just what we expect to have happen will. Our expectations create our realities, and through our own choosing we create our character, and our character creates our destiny. Even though this is an easy concept to state it is a hard concept to understand, internalize, and put into action.

If we consider the polarities of life–north pole-south pole, in-out, yes-no, negative-positive, emotion-knowledge, fear-faith, man-woman, night-day, and on and on, a person could wonder if both are not needed to appreciate one over the other. And, the answer is "yes." In choosing the good, we must acknowledge the bad. In lighting a candle, we must witness the darkness. In appreciating laughter, we must know what it is to cry. Likewise, if we wish to be positive we must overtly turn against the negative side of life.

In teaching children to choose, it is necessary for them to understand the consequences of their choices. If saying "be good" was sufficient to make children comply the world would be an easy place in which to live. Sometimes children and adults are rewarded for bad behavior and repeat behaviors that will bring attention, care and concern, and special consideration to them. It is not a good practice to reap these types of consequences for bad behaviors and parents need to pay attention to this. Rewards should exist for right choices, but not those choices wherein a child manipulates the outcome.

Napoleon Hill has stated that the Universe hates inactivity and a vacuum. A good practice that leads to the rewards of life might be to become actively engaged in filling your mission in life! Just by taking positive steps in the direction of your own choosing, and doing something to fill an empty space you encounter along the way, could lead you to life's rewards. Didn't all of history's "Greats" do this? Could it really be as simple as finding a need and filling it? I believe so.

Your homework for this week is to advance to the reward side of life by discovering a need and filling it. You can start with your dog's water bowl and possibly advance to what a friend of mine is doing tomorrow evening–giving a loving homily by request at her friend's funeral service. Admitting that she has never done this before, Annedia still plans on doing the best job she can in sharing moments from her friend's life that can help others recall the beauty of a life that has both remarkable and sad moments. Whatever it is you decide to pursue, remember not to let life's penalties weigh you down. Rather let life's rewards take you to a new level of performance. You will be rewarded for it with compounded interest!

Which Will You Choose?
by Napoleon Hill

There are two things which nature discourages and severely penalizes:
  (a) a vacuum (emptiness) and
  (b) idleness (lack of action).

Remove any muscle of the body from active use, and it will atrophy (waste away) and become useless. Tie an arm to your side and remove it from action and in time it, too, will wither and become useless. The same law which governs other portions of the body governs the brain, where the vibrations of thought are organized and released.

A positive mind finds a way it can be done,
a negative mind looks for all the ways it can't be done.

You either use your brain for controlled thinking in connection with things you want, or nature steps in and uses it to grow a crop of negative circumstances you do not want. You have a choice in this situation: You can take possession of your thought power, or you can let it be influenced by the stray winds of chance and circumstances you do not desire. But you cannot sit idly by and thus free yourself from the influence of these two sealed envelopes.

Nature allows you to fix your mind on whatever you desire. Nature also allows you to create your own plan for attaining your desire. She crowns all your efforts with those benefits which come in the sealed envelope labeled Rewards. But she discourages idleness and penalizes it wherever it exists.

Out of this truth has grown the saying: *Success attracts more success while failure attracts more failure*–a truth which you may have observed many times although you may not have analyzed why it happens this way.

If you put your mind to work with a positive mental attitude and believe in success as your right, your belief will guide you unerringly toward whatever your definition of success may be. If you adopt a negative mental attitude and fill your mind with thoughts of fear and frustration, your mind will attract to you the penalties of these undesirable thoughts.

Or you may make no attempt to control and direct your mind, opening it wide to every influence with which you come in contact, and it will yield you the things listed in the second sealed envelope, which are the Penalties you must pay for your neglect to possess and direct your mind.

137

Now let us open these two sealed envelopes and see what they contain:

REWARDS
(For those who take possession of their minds and direct them toward desirable objectives.)

a. The privilege of placing yourself on the success beam which attracts only the circumstances which make for success.
b. Sound health, both physically and mentally.
c. Financial independence.
d. A labor of love in which to express yourself.
e. Peace of mind.
f. Applied faith which makes fear impossible.
g. Enduring friendships.
h. Longevity and a well balanced life.
i. Immunity against all forms of self-limitation
j. The wisdom to understand yourself and others.

PENALTIES
(To be paid by those who neglect to take possession of their minds and direct them toward desirable objectives.)

a. Poverty and misery all your life.
b. Mental and physical ailments of many kinds.
c. Self-limitations which bind you to mediocrity all the days of your life.
d. Fear, in all its destructive forms.
e. Dislike of the occupation by which you earn a living.
f. Many enemies, few friends.
g. Every brand of worry known to mankind.
h. A victim of every negative influence you encounter.
i. Subjection to the influence and control of other people at their will.
j. A wasted life which gives nothing to the betterment of mankind.

These lists comprise the catalog of Rewards and Penalties. Which of these lists will you choose as your lot in life?

Source: *PMA Science of Success Course*. Pgs. 221, 222 & 223.

GOOD ^{AS} GOLD
30

I heard it explained this way before, "Morally speaking, if you have to wonder if something is right or wrong, chances are–It's WRONG."
—Greg Reid

Does making a decision hold you back from succeeding? Are you a procrastinator when it comes to deciding how to proceed? Do you continue to weigh the pros and cons of a certain outcome? Are you stuck in the middle of the decision making process? If you are anxious, stressed, scatter-brained, and unable to focus, you are in need of a thorough makeover in how to make a decision and live with the outcome. Correct this flaw in your personality profile, and you will become a stronger version of your former self.

Napoleon Hill identified inability to make a decision as a critical factor in failing to succeed. He states that one of the major causes of lack of success is the "failure to reach decisions promptly and definitely when all the facts necessary for a decision are at hand." After you have assembled all the necessary information and categorized it as "important" or "unimportant" relative to the decision being considered, right then and there you need to make a decision and not look back. It's like driving a car. When you decide to head south it is impossible to make any headway if minute by minute you keep putting the car in reverse. The best you can do in this type of situation is to lurch ahead inch by inch only to be stalled eventually on the highway of life.

Decide to make a decision right now. Establish a reasonable timeline. Gather the information. Categorize the information. Review your findings. Make a decision. It has been said that making a decision, even if it is the wrong one, is better than not deciding. This simple fact is true because you have moved from being a fence sitter to being a bridge maker. When you decide, you garner the forces of the universe in your favor. You become like a magnet drawing to yourself the resources to manifest your decision. I wonder what it is you will decide? After all is said and done, you are the person in control of your decisions. Decisions create outcomes. Decide to create some good ones.

Promptness of Decision
by Napoleon Hill

Observe people wherever you will and you will notice that those who cannot make up their minds are neither popular nor successful. How charmed are you by the personality of a friend who cannot decide whether he, or she, would like to participate with you in some form of activity? Such a person puts you at a real disadvantage. You have invited his participation and are yourself sincere about wanting to do whatever it is you have in mind. By his indecision he prohibits you from securing another partner in the venture, and leaves you in the uncomfortable position of not knowing whether or not you will be able to go ahead with your plans.

Promptness of decision is a very important factor in the attainment of a pleasing personality, and it is a very prominent trait in all successful persons. It is a habit which can be acquired through self-discipline. Promptness of decision develops as a result of a confident, constructive, sure and progressive positive mental attitude. It is closely related, as you will readily perceive, to definiteness of purpose, the starting point of all achievement.

,We live in a country where individual achievement is

140

possible on a grand scale because of the great abundance of opportunities in every calling. But opportunity waits for no man. The man with the vision to recognize opportunity and the promptness of decision necessary to embrace it will get ahead.

Source: *PMA Science of Success Course*. Pgs. 169 & 170.

GOOD ^{AS} GOLD
31

As we also know, there is a difference between wishing for something and being ready to receive or acquire it. The difference? Belief. Until you believe something is possible, it isn't.

— Richard Krasney

Nothing ever just happens. You have to make things happen, including individual success. Success it the direct result of definite action, carefully planned and persistently carried out by the person who has conditioned his mind for success and believes he will attain it.

— Napoleon Hill

Magic Keys to Success (Using the Hill Principles)

1. **Throw the right switch** – (Positive Mental Attitude) Always the **right** mental attitude in any circumstance. Stone's principle of choice. A good mental image to hold in your mind is that nothing will see the light of day until you throw the switch! Let your little light shine.

2. **Show up–even unprepared** – (Go the Extra Mile–GEM of a principle) Carnegie's principle of choice. He states that it made him the business success that he was. Abraham Lincoln wrote the Gettysburg Address on the back of an envelope one hour before he delivered it, but his **LIFE** was present in every word. It has been said many times over

that victory oftentimes goes to those who show up! Most importantly–Show up for life every day!

3. **Don't Share** – i.e., problems. Share solutions. (Teamwork and Mastermind Alliance) Be a "yes, and . . ." person, not a "yes, but. . . ." person when presented with a new idea. No one is really interested in hearing about your unsolved problems. They only become engaged when they see you surmounting insurmountable problems by putting creative solutions to work. Focus on the "can do" part.

4. **Provide Catnip** – Anticipate don't worry. (Creative Visioning) Involve your senses. This technique can be the key to unlocking memories. Thomas Edison was not 20 minutes proving the value of the incandescent light bulb, but he spent decades of his lifetime looking for the correct filament. By providing encouragement to those around you through creative tidbits or "goodies" with the promise of more to come upon the completion of good work, you will engage the hearts and souls of those committed to working with you. And, this works for you too. Hedge your bets–build in some incremental reward in order to get and keep yourself motivated toward achieving your goal.

5. **Be Joyful** – Joy eradicates sadness just as light dispels darkness. (Applied Faith) Remember, fear is faith in reverse. Laugh, joke, and allow the inside massage of laughter to make you feel more alive and vibrant from the inside out.

6. **Ask how to help** – give to give not give to get. (Cosmic Habitforce) Be courteous. Invoke Emerson's Law of Compensation. What goes around comes around. Give away something today to someone who needs it–maybe just a smile or a compliment, but give it freely and consciously. No strings attached.

7. **Hold on to a dream** – (Definite Major Purpose) Where is the magic? It's inside you. Probably the place you would least likely look. Dr. Hill's Principle of Choice–Definite Major Purpose. Locate your dream, cuddle it, formulate a plan to bring it forth, and then unveil it for the world to be part of the plan.

Position yourself on the right (PMA) side of your mind. Feel the spirit of a dream inside you (smell the catnip), and your success will follow as surely as spring follows the winter. "If winter comes, can spring be far behind?" We all see the wondrous nature of the external creation, why not now make it so in our own little world of wonder?

What Constitutes Genius?
by Napoleon Hill

Any dominating desire, plan or purpose which is backed by faith is taken over by the subconscious mind and acted upon immediately.

The mind, stimulated by dominating desire, draws power directly from the subconscious, and, when reinforced by the power of faith, is able to create a conviction of such force that it completely rejects the idea of a possibility of failure. This constitutes genius. And genius is that which may be developed by any person in possession of his or her normal mental faculties.

A good many people have the mistaken idea that there are certain types of people in this world who can be called geniuses. The ingredients which make up genius have been discovered in the last forty years and it is now known that those persons often alluded to as possessing a rare genius actually do not have any powers which you do not possess. They are invariably persons who are consciously and subconsciously following certain basic principles which are responsible for their apparently abnormal power. The following are the basic ingredients of genius, as determined from an extensive analysis of the lives of outstanding men of this nation.

The first ingredient is the subject of this entire lesson–definiteness of purpose. A genius knows what he wants from life. Today's geniuses are busy at the moment, moving directly, with little waste motion, toward accomplishing their objectives.

The second factor is applied faith. Not just a general faith, but applied faith, faith that is concentrated upon the attainment of the definite purpose. Definiteness of purpose is the foundation upon which all faith is based.

The third factor is something that is contagious; it is called enthusiasm, and you should catch some of this. Enthusiasm is the expression of a certain dynamic vitality in the way you walk, talk, and act. It is the result of your motivation and your physical magnetism and energy. It is the light in your eye, the vibrant timbre of your voice, the vigor of your handshake. It is the element which can really build a fire under your desire and make it literally a burning desire. It is a quality which must be controlled and turned on and off at the right time.

The fourth ingredient is imagination, the activity of the mind that makes possible the creation of new ideas. Without imagination nothing new would ever be created. It, too, must be controlled and directed. It is usually most productive when activated by a specific aim or issue.

The fifth factor is motive. You are familiar with the ten basic motives previously discussed. No sane person does anything without a motive; there has to be a reason back of every act.

The sixth factor is personal initiative, backed by intense action. You will never be a genius unless you get into the habit of doing what should be done without waiting for someone to tell you to do it. Personal initiative is the self-starter and it must be kept in perfect shape for instant use. Another way of defining personal initiative might be: The ability to see things as they are and to do things as they should be done.

The seventh factor is the habit of going the extra mile. You will never be a genius unless you make it a habit to do more and better than you are paid to do, every single day of your life.

The eighth factor is forming a master mind alliance with other people. The number in the alliance depends on what you want to accomplish. For your goal in life you may not require more than a dozen or a half-dozen–maybe only one; but if you are going to be a genius you will have to learn to use other people's brain power.

The ninth factor and last is perhaps the most important of all. You may have guessed it. It is a positive mental attitude. You certainly will never rank as a genius until you can positivize your mind and keep it that way at will. Without a positive mental attitude, none of the other ingredients of genius will be available to you.

Source: *PMA Science of Success Course:* Pgs. 29 & 30.

GOOD AS GOLD
32

No matter where we are or what the situation, it is always important to show others our kindness. You'll never know what a huge difference it will make and how far it will take you in life, until you try it.

–Kip Davis

Does trying to be kind ever backfire on you? Are you either snubbed in your efforts or taken advantage of? Do people reject your help or treat you as if being their servant is your destined role in life? If so, how do you know when and where to draw the line so that you are not becoming a well-used doormat?

Wanting to help, supplying the right kind of help, and not overwhelming the recipient are three things you should take into consideration before embarking on your quest to do good deeds. Before giving, it is important to understand the nature of this process from the recipient's perspective. Let's examine the three steps required in providing kindness for the benefit of others and also for ourselves.

1. **Why do you want to help?** In answering this question, make certain that your motive is truly altruistic and does not have a hidden agenda. Too many times people have selfish motives behind their desire to do good, and this negates the "karma" that can be generated by unselfish motives. For example, if you are providing a kindness for an immediate personal gain, your kindness is diminished

because the recipient does not receive the full advantage of your generosity. By looking first at **What's In It For Me?**, you do not give to give, but give to get. By always thinking first of the recipient and how you are helping them, ideally you should be able to eliminate any selfish motives or at least make them secondary.

2. **What's the right kind of help?** Looking at things solely from your perspective can get you into trouble. What might be correct for you may be totally wrong for someone else. For example, when you presume that someone needs your help it is best to check first to see if they really do. When preferences are considered many times people simply prefer to do things their own way rather than your way. Take driving for instance. You might prefer the interstate for the sake of arriving quickly at a destination, but your companion might prefer the side roads in order to enjoy the scenery and relaxed nature of the drive. Whose way is correct? Both are. If you drive a friend somewhere as a favor, consider going by their route instead of yours. Then, you both may benefit from the ride.

3. **Are you overwhelming the recipient?** Everyone's internal clock is different. What may seem timely and opportune on your watch may seem totally incongruous for someone else. Gauge your kindness by the recipient's response. Don't smother a person with your generosity because it feels good to you. Rather, take your cue from the person on the receiving end. If enough is indicated, then stop. Don't forge ahead because then you are not being kind, you are being pushy and pushy equals self-centeredness not kindness. Know when enough is enough.

As you apply these little rules of thumb before acting out your generosity, you will be acting in the person's best interest, not yours. And, that is kindness in action. As the saying goes, "To have a friend, be one."

Effective Stimulants
by Napoleon Hill

Friendship of others can be a great stimulant. There are those who think best by talking problems over with others. Friendship can be a source of new ideas, varied outlook and intellectual and moral support. As a source of laughter, it is a potent stress inhibitor. Laughter trickles through the entire body and tickles every cell into renewed vitality.

A close, warm relationship between parent and child has a most astounding influence in connection with the formation of a child's character. It is regrettable that parents are not able to give more time and energy to develop such a relationship.

The friendship which sometimes exists between the lover of wild life and wild birds and animals is something which is most profound. Most of the creatures of the wild instinctively recognize the lover of wild life and voluntarily show their confidence in him.

The word friendship has more behind it than the mere social relationship of people. Friendship serves to bring the souls of men closer to one another. It builds confidence, inspires courage, enthusiasm, imagination and personal initiative, as nothing else can do.

Mastermind alliances are powerful mind stimulants. Evidence of this is shown in the fact that there are more successful men in all walks of life who have such an alliance.

The potential power which may be attained through the mastermind principle, is shown to the extent that it brings together the minds of many individuals and concentrates their combined power upon the attainment of a definite end. It also provides the means by which the other sixteen principles of this philosophy may be organized and directed as a single force for the attainment of any desired end.

The mastermind principle is the medium through which stimuli from many minds may be combined, and directed to a definite end. Hence, it is among the greatest of the mind stimuli.

Mutual suffering, in times of great emergency, provides

a mind stimulant of stupendous proportions. Mutual suffering has the effect of causing people to consolidate their mind power, through the mastermind principle, and direct it to the alleviation of their suffering.

Autosuggestion is the medium through which every individual stimulates his mind continuously. Unfortunately most of the stimuli which reach the mind of the average person by self-suggestion are of a negative nature. They consist of thoughts of the conditions and things which one does not want—fears, worries, hatreds, envy, greed and superstition.

Source: *PMA Science of Success.* Pgs. 455 & 456.

GOOD AS GOLD
33

Each and every day we really only have one choice to make. And that choice is: Am I doing or saying this from love or fear?

—Brad Justice

It is not too late in the year to review your goals and consider what progress you have made. Today is as auspicious a time to begin something new as the New Year was. Why not give yourself a little push forward by taking action on some languishing goal that you have been nursing along but not really infusing with intensity of purpose? It doesn't have to be a huge push forward, just some immediate action to propel you along on the road to success. It might be a game that you play with yourself that could be as simple as depositing loose change into a piggy bank designated for a special vacation, or it could be the opening of a new savings account wherein you would tithe a portion of your weekly salary to fund a distant dream. Big or small, if you begin today, your goal will be fulfilled that much sooner. Challenge yourself to step into your future by taking action daily to bring a goal closer to reality.

"If you fail to plan you plan to fail," is a saying that should be mulled over. Planning is not necessarily hard work, but many people fail to plan because they dread putting pen to paper. By the very act of writing something down you begin to evolve from the wishing stage to the doing stage. This simple action puts your subconscious mind on notice that you are affirming your goal and expect something to happen. Through goal planning and visualization, you create a pattern of behavior that when repeated creates a niche in your brain that leads you to your ultimate objective. It may take a hundred or a thousand repetitions, but when it does occur it will appear as if it were spontaneous. In retrospect you knew that it would happen all along, but first you had to plant, nurture, and grow the idea in the confines of your subconscious mind before it could fully blossom into reality.

Here's a little idea from a poem that Napoleon Hill quotes. Grab the oars, set sail, and ordain your destiny.

> *I shall not wait the coming of my ship*
> *That's sailing onward through some unknown sea,*
> *But build myself a craft, and through the drip*
> *I'll go a-sailing outward, sturdily,*
> *Until I reach the ports where I shall find*
> *The cargoes other folks are waiting for,*
> *And gather in what gain the tide and wind*
> *Hold for the wight that dares to leave the shore.*
>
> —John Kendrick Bangs

Your Independence Fund
by Napoleon Hill

Here is a story about a young man who couldn't get any response from his employer in spite of his continued best efforts to apply the principle of going the extra mile and practicing the Golden Rule. The young man wisely decided to tell his employer to get someone to take his place. But a depression was on, and he couldn't afford to do this until he had saved some money. For one whole year he and his wife pinched and saved until they had a couple thousand dollars in the bank. Then he did exactly what he had been planning to do during that long year of self-denial.

That young man went out and secured other capital and went into business for himself, as a competitor of his former boss. And he made good. Now he has a tradition in his plant that every new employee must come in to him for a personal interview before going to work. During this interview he relates the story of how he got his start in business. He tells the new employee: "If you have the kind of stuff in you that we think you have and hope you have, the time will inevitably come when you will have the urge to tell me you are through, and, of course, that will mark the parting of our ways. Now, I want you to be prepared to do just that when the feeling gets so strong you can't resist it, so I want you to start a savings account immediately and see that a percentage of your salary goes into it every payday. You may call it your independence fund, and that will make it more fun to save."

You could search in vain, the world over, for a more harmonious group of employees, with a real respect for their boss. They all have a private independence fund and are in a position to break off any time conditions warrant such a move. But the boss knows this, and treats his employees with the respect that is due them, so he will not lose his valuable men. He sees to it that he does not give them any legitimate excuse for leaving him.

This story gives a slight twist to the principle of going the extra mile because of a mutual feeling of independence and pride. The result is high output per man, increased profits for the company, higher wages for employees, and a company organization that no "ism" except Americanism can penetrate.

Source: *PMA Science of Success Course.* Pgs. 153 & 154.

GOOD AS GOLD
34

Sports officials and referees, by the very nature of their vocation, should be exemplary students of Dr. Hill.

–Rich Winograd

As a nation, the United States of America is very good at turning failure and adversity into an asset. The future of the nation is not determined by the defeats experienced, but rather by the failures overcome. There is a lesson in every defeat. As a nation we advance when we learn not only how to weather the storm but how to profit from it.

The same holds true for our own shortcomings. There is a lesson in each and every adversity. When something goes wrong the best response is one where we stand toe to toe with defeat and look it squarely in the face. We may even recognize the "enemy" but a known adversary is better than a spectral one. Once we put a name to the face, we can then begin to address how the situation can be remedied.

Part of the learning from adversity and defeat is inherent in the cause of the misfortune. If we know the cause we can predict the outcome. The current situation may be past intervention, but future ones are open to actions that could change the result from negative to positive. For this reason alone, it is good to examine our defeats for the purpose of changing our pattern of results.

Historically, countries that survive examine their choices. Future mistakes can be avoided, and the past can be a learning experience not a death sentence. By changing the dominating thoughts of your mind, you can turn the tide in your favor and an entire country can do the same. As our awareness increases, so do our responses. What was once habitual and conditioned, can become thoughtful and advanced. When one person decides to stop and think, many others may follow suit and a higher consciousness is born.

To begin, consider the choices that you make. Are they random, habitual, or thoughtful ones? When a choice is thoughtful, we are able to connect our thinking with our destiny. This is no small awareness. Knowing that what we think about we become, not only can change our life, but the lives of all those on this planet. We can think our way to a better future through weathering one defeat after another and analyzing why it happened in the first place. Think first, act second is a good axiom to follow. Try putting it into practice. Your life will show the difference.

Failure and Adversity
by Napoleon Hill

Failure and adversity have introduced many men to opportunities which they would not have recognized under more favorable circumstances.

A man's mental attitude in respect to defeat is the factor of major importance in determining whether he rides with the tides of fortune on the success side of the River of Life or is swept to the failure side by circumstances of misfortune.

The circumstances which separate failure from success often are so slight that their real cause is overlooked. Often they exist entirely in the mental attitude with which one meets temporary defeat. The man with a positive mental attitude reacts to defeat in a spirit of determination not to accept it. The man with a negative mental attitude reacts to defeat in a spirit of hopeless acceptance.

The man who maintains a positive mental attitude may have anything in life upon which he may set his heart, so long as it does not conflict with the laws of God and the rights of his fellowmen. He probably will experience many defeats, but he will not surrender to defeat. He will convert it into a stepping stone from which he will rise to higher and higher areas of achievement.

The subject of a positive mental attitude is so important that it not only claimed first position in the list of the twelve riches of life, but it had to be included as an important part of the principle on pleasing personality, and has been mentioned in practically every principle of this course.

A positive mental attitude is an essential part of the key which unlocks the door to the solution of all personal problems. It is the magic quality of this key which enables it to attract success as surely as an electro-magnet attracts iron filings.

The whole secret of the formula by which you may turn defeat into an asset lies in your ability to maintain a positive mental attitude despite your defeat.

Source: *PMA Science of Success Course*: Pgs. 395 & 396.

GOOD ^{AS} GOLD
35

I learned to make the goal specific and small. Just do it one step at a time and achieve it SLIGHTLY.

–Hansong Zhang

As you are well aware, Napoleon Hill's philosophy is international in scope and distribution. Daily, I am reminded of this as Guang Chen, my technical assistant, reports to work. Born in Shanghai, China, he now lives with his wife Jing in Hammond, Indiana as she completes her graduate studies here at Purdue University Calumet. Alan "Guang" Chen has been working for the Napoleon Hill World Learning Center since he too was a graduate student in engineering. On campus this semester we have hundreds of Chinese students who are working toward degrees and also learning simultaneously about our American culture. Many of these students study Dr. Hill's philosophy because they were introduced to the Principles of Success in China and are pleased to see it offered here as well.

One such student is Hansong. Hansong is an eager student when it comes to advanced learning, and he also is a graduate of several of our courses. It is his goal to learn as much as he can about all self-help motivational philosophies. He works hard to internalize the teachings of Dr. Hill into his everyday life. By extracting the essence of the philosophy, Hansong is able to match up his eastern culture with western thought. I can't help but think that he is accumulating riches that he will use for the rest of his life. I was amazed at his integration of ideas concerning what Dr. Hill's teachings bring to an individual. Not only is he bright and educated, he is also practical in his approach to life.

With Alan teaching our Chinese students the Keys to Success course in their native language, these young people are preparing for a life that is rich and full. It is an advantage that I wish would be sought out by all students. It doesn't matter that much of Hill's philosophy is viewed as common sense, what matters is that we not only understand it but apply it. Maybe that is what gives one country over another a leading edge.

In this global economy and world at large everyone would be well served if they practiced a little common sense, a little common courtesy, and a little of the common touch that leads to a truly uncommon life. Hansong and Alan have found the principles that serve them on their road to success. What about other young people? Isn't it time that someone sits them down and discusses these principles with them? Maybe you can start at home, and then expand to your local community. If each one teaches one, the philosophy will expand exponentially and the world will become a better place by reaching one attentive student at a time.

An Important Caution
by Napoleon Hill

Keep your specific goal in life and your plans for achieving it strictly to yourself. Do not talk about it or tell anyone about it except the members of your master mind alliance, and, of course, your instructor. One reason for this secrecy is that continually talking about your objective and plans to those not really interested in them will dissipate your power. Here's a little jingle to remember: *The steam that makes the whistle blow will never make the engine go.*

Take a look at a teakettle boiling away on a kitchen range. It is sizzling away its power. If you could cork up the spout and fasten down the lid, the accumulated steam pressure would soon blow the whole thing apart. You must get up steam behind your purposes and plan, and avoid sizzling it away aimlessly in idle chatter.

Another reason–and an even more important one–for keeping quiet about what you intend to do, is that to disclose your plans to those who are not in sympathy with you, gives them the very ammunition they need to defeat you. People prompted by jealousy, envy, and other negative thoughts will seize with delight any opportunity to make fun of you and your definite aim. Do not permit them to enjoy themselves at your expense. Avoid exposure to their discouraging negative influence. Unfortunately, the members of your own immediate family may sometimes be the very ones who will take advantage of your confidence and discourage your ideas for self-improvement.

There are people in this world who have nothing better to do than stand on the side lines of life and stick out their feet just to see others tumble, and if they learn which way you're going, they may be lying in wait for you. If you don't tell them in what direction you are heading, they won't be there to cause your downfall. Remember to call your specific goal in life and your plans for achieving it into your consciousness as often as may be practical. Eat with them; sleep with them; and take them with you wherever you go. Bear in mind the fact that your subconscious mind can thus be influenced to work for the attainment of your goal while you are asleep. *Keep your mind on the things you want and off the things you don't want!*

Source: *PMA Science of Success Course.* Pgs. 44 & 45.

GOOD ᴬˢ GOLD
36

Giving starts with how you serve those who work inside your organization, and then radiates out to others you serve as part of your mission.

–John Hope Bryant

This business about giving before you get continues to startle and confuse many people. Often I am asked the question as to how this is possible. People continually state that they cannot give before they receive because they have no savings from which to draw from for their charitable contributions. They argue that they must build up a large reserve prior to making any type of contribution to the charity or program of their choice. When asked to contribute from their current funds they become even more adamant about waiting until they have a surplus from which to draw. This fosters the need to hoard rather than a need to create a prosperous flow from which everyone benefits.

The Napoleon Hill World Learning Center has been the recent recipient of donated funds from OrGano Gold International with the public promise of greater donations to follow. They are espousing the philosophy of "paying it forward" and have even incorporated this concept into their mission as an organization. For them, it is not "when" they arrive at their financial goal, but "right now" as they build their company. This "principles coupled with profit" or values-based leadership is not a unique concept in theory, but it is in practice. Instead of drawing from their reserve, the OrGano Gold organization is gifting from their immediate bottom line with the intention of making charitable donations an integral part of the mission of their company. Giving is not an afterthought, but an actual tenet of their action plan as stated in their published mission. It is their belief that giving before getting stimulates the flow of business and compensates everyone in the end in a greater way than giving from excess or reserve does.

Napoleon Hill states this very concept in his philosophy of success. When creating your success plan in the six steps he outlines in *Think and Grow Rich,* Dr. Hill states that you must give prior to receiving, and you must also give in proportion to that which you hope to receive. How many people can you name who do this? If you can name anyone, you might also consider the level of their success. Remember, success is achieved though a balance. Financial riches are only one indication of success. And, other indications such as peace of mind, a positive mental attitude, sound physical health, and harmony in human relationships all rank above financial security.

Let's keep our vision clear and focused and chart our course not by what we hope to receive but by what we contribute.

The Privilege of Rendering
an Overplus of Service
by Napoleon Hill

Henry Ford once told about a young man who came to him for a position, and while they were discussing his salary, the young man would not set a definite figure; he seemed undecided. Mr. Ford made the suggestion that he come to work and that he would be paid, at the end of the month, just what he was worth. The young man blurted out: "But I'm already getting more than that!" No doubt he told the truth that time.

You must do that for which you are paid to keep your job, *but you have the privilege of rendering an overplus of service as a means of accumulating a reserve credit of good will which entitles you to higher pay and a better position! If no such overplus is rendered,* you have not a single argument in your favor when you ask for a better position and increased pay. Think this over for yourself and you will have the real answer to why it pays to go the extra mile.

It is important to point out the all-too-common mistake of confusing your financial *needs* with your demand for wages. If you have extravagant habits and manage your money matters so poorly that you cannot live on the salary you make, consider carefully that, perhaps, you are now receiving the full value of the service you are rendering. Remember that both employers and employees must observe certain fundamentals of economics. Certain types of service carry corresponding maximum wages, which it is economically unsound to exceed. If the type of service you are trained to render does not bring the compensation you feel that you require, then you should consider a change in occupation. If you like the work you're doing, perhaps there is some area of it wherein you can render an extra amount of service and thus justify your expectation of increased earnings. One thing is sure: *If you never do anything more than you are paid to do, you'll never get paid for anything more than you do.*

Source: *PMA Science of Success Course.* Pgs. 158 & 159.

GOOD ^{AS} GOLD

37

The bigger the desire of the new habit or change is, the faster the subconscious is responsible to have that desired behavior transformed into unconscious habit.

–Francisco Mendoza

There is a poem entitled "My Kingdom" by Lousia May Alcott that reads as follows:

My Kingdom
A little kingdom I possess,
    Where thoughts and feelings dwell;
And very hard the task I find
    Of governing it well . . .
I do not ask for any crown
    But that which all may win;
Nor try to conquer any world
    Except the one within.

Upon reflection, this poem reminds us that before we can get the world right, we must get the man right, before we can change the world, we must change ourselves and before we can govern others we must first demonstrate the capacity to be in command of ourselves.

Each of us is a potential ruler in our own kingdom and our subjects to be ruled are our passions, desires, and fears. When this is accomplished, we can truly say that we are rulers of the world–our little personalized world that we alone inhabit all the days of our life. And that is absolutely the most important world that we live in because if we are not content, happy, productive, and nourishing to ourselves, how can we be so to another?

As we look within, we better understand the philosophy of success. Dr. Hill states: "With a determined will power you can shut the door on any unwanted memories, and open the door of opportunity in any direction of your own choice. If you find the first door hard to open, you will try another, and so on, until you find one where you may enter." He goes on to add, "Definiteness of purpose is the starting point of everything that man achieves. Will power, under self-discipline, keeps man going until he accomplishes his purposes. You now have the key. What will you do with it?"

Dr. Hill always reminds us that when we are ready for the "secret" the master key will appear. Could the hidden key be as simple as self-discipline? Does this one principle unlock the door to success? Just check the record on any success story and see if the person you are researching exercised self-discipline. I don't think you will be surprised at what you find out. This one principle could be your master key to success! But, only if you use it!

Uncontrollable Elements of the Thinking Process
by Napoleon Hill

There are four elements of the thinking process which cannot be controlled directly by the individual. You can adapt yourself to them, but you cannot control them.

First of these is Infinite Intelligence. This will be further explained in the principle of Cosmic Habitforce. You cannot discipline Infinite Intelligence. According to the best evidence available, it is the source of all thought energy.

The subconscious mind. This part of the mind is not subject to control by the individual. It is the connecting link between the conscious mind of man and Infinite

170

Intelligence. No one can discipline it. It works in its own way . . . its major function being that of appropriating and acting upon the dominating thoughts of the conscious mind.

One peculiar characteristic of the subconscious mind is that it will not take orders from the conscious mind. It acts only upon order of the emotions. This is one more reason for acquiring self-discipline over the emotions. The subconscious mind will carry out the instructions of the negative emotions just as quickly as it will respond to the positive. It makes no attempt to distinguish between these. The only control you have over the subconscious is gained by exercising self-discipline to impress your subconscious mind with your definite major purpose.

The third uncontrollable department of the mind is the sixth sense, or telepathy. This is the broadcasting and receiving station for messages which travel at vibratory rates above those perceived by the regular senses. It is obviously not subject to control except to a limited extent when the mind is stimulated by a master mind association.

The fourth uncontrollable department consists of the five normal senses of seeing, smelling, tasting, hearing and touching. They may deceive you. Examples of this can be found in motion pictures, feats of magic and the speedy draw of the cowboy, when the hand is quicker than the eye. It is necessary constantly to check the findings of these extensions of the mental faculties by submitting them to the presiding judge in the court of reason. They are disciplined by voluntary habits.

Source: *PMA Science of Success Course.* Pgs. 289 & 290.

GOOD AS GOLD
38

Albert Einstein once said, "when a person is sufficiently motivated discipline will take care of itself."

—Justin Savich

It is good to get the entire picture of just what Dr. Hill's philosophy contains so that we can be reminded that in order to succeed at our highest level we need to incorporate each and every principle into our life. The mainstays of Definiteness of Purpose, Mastermind Alliance, Applied Faith and Going the Extra Mile are the essential ingredients, but the 13 remaining principles cannot be overlooked if we want to achieve utmost effectiveness. They are more than icing on the cake. They are each as essential as the Big Four, and serve to complement and enhance the others.

In schools today the buzzword is experiential learning. As you probably know, there is really nothing new under the sun. Experiential learning is simply learning tied to doing or what I like to refer to as application. Learning to do through application ties the lesson to the learner in the same manner that a boat or ship is moored to a dock. This anchor serves as a connecting link to whatever outcome you desire to achieve. As we all know, repetition is the key! Repetition creates habit, and our habits create our destiny.

The problem we encounter in real life is how do we make something that is philosophical also pragmatic and useful in our workaday lives? Dr. Hill tells us that the answer is in attaching the emotions to the outcome, but that too can present a problem unless we can conjure up our emotions easily.

In consideration of the above, I have created a learning tool together with my team that combines the success principles with music and visuals in a thirty minute meditation tutorial. Artist Mike Telapary and Concert Pianist Antonio Castillo de la Gala are paired together by design consultant Chris Lake with Dr. Hill's description of each of the 17 Principles, and the result is magical.

I guarantee that if you quietly sit in front of your computer and listen to and watch this meditation attentively once each day for 21 consecutive days, you will be emotionally moved by what is presented. Let your mind go into a comforting, meditative state and allow the information to fill your mind, becoming part of your consciousness first and, over time, your subconscious. I suggest either doing the meditation first thing in the morning or the last thing at night. Experience it privately without interruption. Allow yourself to become part of both the melody and images so that you can harmonize with the principles in the real world.

Interested? All sales of the **Meditation on the Principles of Success** benefit the Napoleon Hill World Learning Center's Education Programs. You can order yours today by contacting Alan Chen, our media specialist. Email him at guangc@hotmail.com. He will help you decide what format will best meet your needs. For the nominal investment of $19.95, the benefit is priceless.

How to Develop Your Burning Desire
by Napoleon Hill

Any dominating idea, plan or purpose held in the conscious mind through repetition of thought and emotionalized by a burning desire for its realization is taken over by the subconscious and acted upon through whatever natural and logical means may be available.

It is significant that the only thing over which you have complete right of control at all times is your own mental attitude. Right of control means that you can control it. It does not mean that you do control it. The purpose of this lesson and others in this series is to teach you how to exercise this right as a matter of habit.

You are somewhat familiar with the concept of the two divisions of the mind–the conscious and the subconscious. Here is a brief explanation: The conscious mind is where reasoning or thinking occurs. It is where deliberation and weighing of facts take place. It is capable of analyzing information and data which come before it, and one of its functions is to act as the guardian of the passageway to the subconscious. The conscious mind is the part of the mind with which you will select your goal in life, as a result of experience. That of newborn infants may be likened to a new recording disc on which are to be recorded the lessons learned through the perceptive avenues of the five senses: seeing, hearing, feeling, smelling, and tasting. You may also compare it to unexposed motion picture film, which is ready to receive the images of perception as they come in through the five senses.

The subconscious mind is the natural uncultivated part of the mind, which comes as standard equipment at birth. It does not think, reason or deliberate. It acts instinctively in response to the basic emotions of humankind, discussed earlier in this lesson. These basic urges to action, or drives, are common to all human beings. They are similar in all persons; that is why we can understand and make use of them. The differences in persons around us are caused by the different ways in which they have trained their conscious minds; subconsciously there is very little individual difference.

To illustrate the power potential of the subconscious mind, we will mention some examples with which you are familiar. The subconscious mind may be likened to an automobile, while the conscious mind may be considered the driver. The power is in the automobile–not the driver.

The driver learns to release and control the power in the motor. In the same way, a person may learn how to tap the power of the subconscious mind and direct it into channels of his own choosing. The conscious mind is the architect; the subconscious mind is the vast storehouse from which may be requisitioned the mental materials for the project which is under construction. The conscious mind makes the plan and decides what shall be done. The subconscious mind develops the power to do it.

None of us really knows very much about the subconscious mind. We do, however, know how it works. We know that we have some characteristic in our mind which acts very much the same way as the sensitized film in a camera. It is capable of receiving any image that is transferred to it by the conscious mind under the influence of a strong emotion. The conscious mind acts as the lens in the mental camera. It collects the light rays reflected by the object of your desire and brings them to a focal point. Getting good pictures with this camera is like getting them with any other–the focus must be sharp, there must be good exposure, and the timing must be right.

Source: *PMA Science of Success*. Pgs. 26, 27, & 28.

GOOD AS GOLD
39

Once I believed that I could become wealthy my mindset shifted.

–Koren Motekaitis

It is good to be literate. If you are literate you can read and extract information from reading materials that are useful for your own life. I believed so much in reading and the positive outcomes that one gains from being able to read and digest material that I became a reading specialist early on in my educational career. I wanted to know everything about helping students to become better readers and to learn how to extract information from a text. I studied a subject called content area reading that illuminated techniques that trained the reader to gather the most meaning from a book, chapter, poem, manual, or whatever was under study. I gained invaluable information that assisted me in being able to glean information from whatever I desired to read. And, most importantly I was able to assist my students in doing the same.

There is also another type of literacy called financial literacy. This is as important as being literate in reading. Financial literacy details the ABCs of getting and keeping the wealth that you earn in your lifetime. Many students are reluctant to learn financial literacy because they may have a notion that they were not meant to be wealthy. Wealth can have a negative connotation when it is not understood properly. Once I had a professional person tell me that he failed to read *Think and Grow Rich* because in his view the title was obnoxious. When I explained to him that the title was meant to stimulate thought and that Dr. Hill was talking about more than financial riches, he decided to rethink his comment. He admitted that his belief kept him from reading a book that went on to change his life.

The Bible states that the "love of money is the root of all evil." Oftentimes, the word "love" is downplayed or left off and people misread the quotation and assume that "money is the root of all evil." Money is not something to be hoarded or squandered. If used wisely and with thought, it can bring about many positive occurrences in the world. Being financially literate is another way of saying that you know the place money has in your life and know how best to use this resource for the good of yourself and others.

First we must understand that all knowledge can be a valuable resource, but only if we know how to apply it. If our life is out of balance, perhaps by acquiring a little education and then applying it will put us on a more even and less rocky path. If you find yourself lacking in an area that seems to elude your understanding, begin first by seeking information from your public library. After you acquire the basics, find a mentor whose advice you can follow. Then, apply what you have learned. Thought plus Action = SUCCESS. As Don Green, Executive Director of the Napoleon Hill Foundation, says, "You have to DO something with what you know." It is in the doing that brings the best results.

Some Tests to Help You
Separate Fact from Fiction
by Napoleon Hill

The accurate thinker scrutinizes everything he reads in books or newspapers, everything he hears and sees over radio and television. He never accepts any statement as fact merely because he has read it or has heard it spoken. And he knows that statements bearing some portion of facts are often intentionally or carelessly colored, modified and exaggerated to give them an erroneous meaning.

Therefore the accurate thinker has definite tests which he applies to the statements of others. If he reads a book, for example, he tests its accuracy by these rules:

   a. Is the writer a recognized authority on the subject covered?
   b. Did the writer have a motive other than that of imparting accurate information when he wrote the book?
   c. Is the writer a professional whose business is that of influencing public opinion?
   d. Has the writer a profit interest in the subjects on which he writes?
   e. Is the writer a person with sound judgment, and not a fanatic on the subject on which he writes?
   f. Are there readily accessible sources from which the writer's statements may be checked and verified?
   g. Do the writer's statements harmonize with common sense and experience?

Before the accurate thinker accepts the statements of others as facts, he tries to find the motive which prompted the statements, for he knows that no one ever does anything, and seldom says anything, without a definite motive. The accurate thinker examines with care all statements made by people who have obvious motives. He is equally careful about accepting the statements of over-zealous people who have the habit of allowing their imaginations to run wild.

Look over carefully the fellow who is trying to sell you his way of life and make sure his way is as good as your own.

Source: *PMA Science of Success* Course: Pgs. 301 & 302.

often intentionally or carelessly omitted, modified, and excerpts all together [illegible] erroneous meaning.

Therefore the critical thinker [illegible] ask himself [illegible] [illegible] [illegible] a book, for example, help us [illegible] presentation:

a. Is the writer a recognized authority on the subject covered?

b. Did the writer [illegible] [illegible] [illegible] [illegible] when [illegible] the book?

c. Is the writer a professional [illegible] [illegible] influencing public opinion?

d. Has the writer any profit interest in the subject on which he writes?

e. Is the writer biased with [illegible] [illegible] and not [illegible]?

f. Are there [illegible] [illegible] [illegible] which the writer [illegible] [illegible]?

g. Is the [illegible] [illegible] [illegible] common [illegible] and [illegible]?

The critical reader [illegible] accepts the statements of [illegible] as facts [illegible] the [illegible] [illegible] [illegible] [illegible] [illegible] [illegible] anything, [illegible] a definite [illegible], the [illegible] [illegible] will [illegible] all statements made by people who have [illegible] motives. He [illegible] [illegible] keeping [illegible] [illegible] of [illegible] people [illegible] [illegible] imagination [illegible] mind.

GOOD AS GOLD
40

Though money may not, in reality, make the world go 'round, it certainly appears to provide the necessary pieces from which our desires are crafted and our dreams fulfilled.

–**Elisabeth Donati**

Everyone loves a bargain, a sale, a wise investment, and money management that makes your income go farther. But, not many people like to practice frugality. For some it seems to have a bad connotation–like "someone" is forcing you to live beneath your means. Could this interpretation be because we were never introduced to the positive aspects of frugality? Just as there can be joy in spending, there can be an equal amount of joy in saving too. Why not give it a try and see for yourself? Make it a game, if that's what it takes to get you focused on this bugaboo of a concept. I have found that when I find a bargain–because I look for one and it turns up–that I revel in the prize, and the real prize is in the savings that I can take to the bank.

For example, I am by my own admission a "book-a-holic." I love books, but do not necessarily like to pay the cover price for current selections. So, I shop the book section at used book stores, Goodwill, the Salvation Army, church sales, garage sales, rummage sales, and library sales. Most times, I find what I am looking for at a fraction of the cost, and other times I find something even better.

Here is a story from my daughter-in-law who is in "frugality" training from her mother-in-law! I enjoyed her story as she tells it below:

Lupita writes:

Dear Judy:

I have a story for you! There is a mirror I have wanted to buy to put it in the dining room. I wanted a big mirror with gold or light brown frame to match with the decor and the dining room furniture. I had a hard time finding one that I liked. I went from a thrift store, to Bed Bath and Beyond, from Macy's to Lowe's...everywhere! Didn't find anything nice, or they were too expensive.

Last night Tim and I went for a run around the neighborhood, and we found a big mirror outside a house among the trash. It was too dark to really see it, but the size seemed about perfect so we took it home. Once we got there, we realized that it was the perfect mirror for the dining room. It is beautiful and it couldn't match better! It is also in great condition. I can't believe I've been looking for it for awhile, and I ended up finding it in someone's trash! I got exactly the mirror I wanted for free!

Love,
Lupita

Personally, I love it when someone can turn trash into treasure! Recycle, reuse, and renew. And, you can take your savings to the bank! And, don't forget, what you look for with intensity and enthusiasm, you find every time.

Frugality
by Napoleon Hill

Frugality is one of the essentials of success. The habit of planned savings encourages frugality, makes it an established habit.

Every man is where he is, and what he is, because of the habits he has acquired. The man who lives up to the limit of his income, or beyond it, never is a free man. He is forever under bondage to others, and bondage is not a welcomed circumstance. It is not part of the Creator's purpose for man.

From here on each of us is under obligation to guard our individual sources and our time as efficiently as a well managed corporation manages its funds and the time of its employees.

If this obligation confuses or irritates some of us, let us take comfort from the fact that it will at least lead us into better habits of self-discipline. And let us recognize that we are approaching the interpretation of a rule of human conduct which is the hope of mankind because it holds the secret by which we may escape from the liabilities of this age of confusion and chaos through which we are passing.

Presentation of this great rule has been reserved as a fitting climax to the principles previously described. It rightly serves as a climax for the sixteen preceding principles because it is the principle which gives moral guidance in the use of the power which the first sixteen principles place into your hands.

Power is a dangerous thing in the hand of someone who does not recognize a moral obligation in its use. The history of mankind proves this.

Source: *PMA Science of Success Course*. Pg. 486.

GOOD AS GOLD
41

The Napoleon Hill Foundation is a not for profit charitable institution which uses the revenues it receives from sales of its books and audios for educational purposes. Its principal activities are funding scholarships, professorships and courses at the University of Virginia at Wise, Virginia and Purdue University-Calumet, and instructing adult and juvenile correctional institution inmates in Dr. Hill's seventeen principles.

–Robert Johnson

While traveling to Wise, Virginia this past weekend for the celebration of Napoleon Hill Day on October 26–which also coincided with Dr. Hill's birthday this year–I anticipated stopping at a remarkable bookstore in Berea, Kentucky. This bookstore stop has become a ritual in our yearly trek to this event. Like kids in a candy store, I and my traveling companions never know what we will find because the store's offerings are a combination of new and used materials. Also, being located in a college town oftentimes makes the mix of choices more interesting too. We were ready to shop.

Being on a tight schedule this year, we hurried into the bookstore with only an hour to spare in our treasure hunt. My two assistants, Chino Martinez and Alan Chen, both scurried to their favorite categories passing by the checkout desk and not seeing the book that was at the cashier's station facing toward the aisle. I stopped, and it was impossible to ignore it since I had seen it many times before.

It was Dr. Hill's famous *Law of Success*. It was a nice thick book with a white paperback cover. Someone had ordered it but it was not our publication. I approached the owner and told him who we were and asked him if it would be too much trouble to sell only authorized books by the Foundation, not unauthorized ones that may also have been modified. He stated that he did not know the difference. So, I told him what to look for and why it was important to the Foundation's longevity to do so. I felt that Dr. Hill had arranged this entire event to remind me once again to ask our legal counsel, Attorney Robert Johnson, to write a guest column outlining the reasons that purchasing only "Foundation Authorized Materials" is so important.

After I accomplished my mission of discussing Dr. Hill's books with the owner, a woman walks up to me and also asks me for my card. She said that she was the person who ordered the book and was just picking it up. She continued to say that she had no idea that there were "authorized" and "unauthorized" versions of Dr. Hill's materials. She gladly promised to do her due diligence and seek out our materials first for future reading. We both left happier knowing that she and the bookstore owner would do exactly as they said. And, I felt that I had just expressed Dr. Hill's wishes in the very place–Berea, Kentucky–where his son attended school. It was like holy Hill ground, and a good place to get his message across to me and the people in Berea.

Arriving at Wise, I met Bob Johnson and asked him to write this week's guest column and he did so before he retired for the night. You can read his column on the website–www.naphill.org. So, as you can see, Dr. Hill must have been asking both of us to remind you, the reader, that before he died he established the Napoleon Hill Foundation with his wife Annie Lou Hill to continue the legacy of his great work. As with any author, it is always best to read the primary work that the author created without commentary and additions or deletions. This gives you, the reader, the opportunity to use your greatest power–your power to choose what you want to think and believe. Afterwards, if you need more information, you can then read the secondary material that has developed around the works. But, read the works themselves first in the purest condition that you can find them in–and that is the materials as Napoleon Hill authored them. By thinking for yourself, you can grow rich, but not by thinking thoughts implanted in your mind by someone else–that is usually called brain-washing. Don't be a sponge, but rather a magnet—an educated reader who reads with pen and notebookin hand–always at the ready–just in case that idea Napoleon Hill promised would surface from your subconscious mind and place you on the fast track to life's riches. Write it down, take action on it, and then make your own dream come true–not someone else's.

You can do it. I know you can.

Thoughts on Success
by Napoleon Hill

Definiteness of Purpose - Successful people move on their own initiative, but they know where they are going before they start.

Mastermind Alliance - No man can become a permanent success without taking others along with him.

Applied Faith - You can do it if you believe you can.

Going the Extra Mile - The most successful people are those who serve the greatest number of people.

Pleasing Personality - It is essential that you develop a Pleasing Personality–pleasing to yourself and others.

Personal Initiative - Today's employer usually is yesterday's employee who found opportunity waiting for him at the end of the second mile.

Positive Mental Attitude - Keep your mind on the things you want and off the things you don't want. Remember the old proverb: "Be very careful what you set your heart on, for you will surely achieve it."

Enthusiasm - To be enthusiastic–act enthusiastically!

Self-Discipline - Direct your thoughts, control your emotions, and ordain your destiny!

Accurate Thinking - Truth will be truth, regardless of a closed mind, ignorance or the refusal to believe.

Controlled Attention - Keep your mind on the things you want and off the things you don't want!

Teamwork - Harmonious cooperation is a priceless asset which you can acquire in proportion to your giving.

Adversity and Defeat - Remember: Every defeat, every disappointment and every adversity carries with it the seed of an equivalent or greater benefit.

Creative Vision - The imagination is the workshop of the soul wherein are shaped all plans for individual achievement.

Maintenance of Sound Health - If you think you're sick, you are.

Budgeting Time and Money - Tell me how you use your spare time and how you spend your money, and I will tell you where and what you will be ten years from now.

Cosmic Habitforce - You are where you are and what you are because of your established habits of thoughts and deeds.

Source: *PMA Science of Success Course* by Napoleon Hill.

GOOD AS GOLD
42

If we define ourselves by what we do, how then do we define ourselves when we stop doing those things?

—Dr. J. B. Hill

October 26 is Dr. Napoleon Hill's birthday. He was born on this date in 1883 and passed away on November 8, 1970. So, in 2009 he would have celebrated his 126th birthday. Could he have imagined that on this date at the University of Virginia's College at Wise, his grandson Dr. J. B. Hill would address two groups of students–one secondary (high school) and one collegiate–as the Keynote Speaker for the Napoleon Hill Foundation? Maybe yes, maybe no. But regardless of this occurrence, Dr. Napoleon Hill knew fully that cosmic habitforce has a hand in all the days of our lives. If asked whether this was a coincidence or not, I believe that he would have answered a firm "no." And, he would go on to state that it was meant to happen because Infinite Intelligence has full knowledge of all the roles and functions that each of us are positioned to play in this life.

Dr. J. B. Hill not only resembles his grandfather physically, but he resembles him intellectually as well. He has inherited the mental acumen that made his grandfather remarkable and an icon in the self-help movement. J. B. is introspective, talented, and degreed, but he is also a lifelong learner, multifaceted, and a good and compassionate listener. He is slow to pronounce an ultimatum and always considerate in his response. All in all, as Shakespeare might phrase it, he resembles a Renaissance Man.

Although a Marine, he personifies the Army slogan, "Be all you can be." When he retired from the Marine Corps after having taught at the Naval Academy, he went on to become an MD and is a practicing physician today.

Who then is the real J. B. Hill? I will let him speak for himself in the guest columns that he will be sharing with us for the next few weeks. For me, J. B. Hill is a person that I am glad I have met because through his acquaintance I have become a better person. For me, that is the true mark of a genuine individual. Not who they are, but what they can inspire you to become. With that said, I believe that he is truly walking in his grandfather's footsteps.

Victim or Victor? You Decide.
by Napoleon Hill

God moves in a mysterious way, His wonders to perform wrote William Cowper in 1772. And if we could only get a long range perspective of the eternal scheme, we could see that these upheavals in our social, political and economic institutions are sent to break up the undesirable mass habits of men. They may be the means of clearing the way for growth and progress in the overall evolution of the race.

Men of great achievement may be playing parts in an overall pattern, or plan, and they may be serving some purpose far beyond their own conception. Take a man like Thomas A. Edison. He probably thought he was inventing to make money, but for all we know, nature may have had another idea. She may have been using him as an instrument for the betterment of all mankind. At least, he did improve the lot of every one of us.

Two great forces are working in the minds of all men to make them what they are. One is social heredity, and the other is physical heredity.

Physical heredity is the law of nature through which the sum and substance of all characteristics, traits and physical

190

aspects of your ancestors, through the ages, have been handed on to you. You are unavoidably a product of all your ancestors.

Social heredity consists of every influence with which you will come in contact, from the time you reach a state of consciousness until you die. Your mother's and father's influence, your education, the conversations you listen to, religious influences, political ideas, the newspapers you read, the shows you see–they all have and will help to make you what you are. They are your social inheritance. Very few persons have what it takes to pull away from these and do some independent, accurate thinking for themselves. A few cast off their social inheritance and dare to be different and individualistic. When this happens, the world has an Edison, a Ford, a Thomas Paine, an Ingersoll or a Jonas Salk. But the vast majority of people allow themselves to become victims of social heredity. This is why straight thinking is such a rarity.

It's a great moment in your life when you break away from your social heredity and start doing your own thinking. Both social and physical heredity are under the direction of cosmic habitforce. Subconscious application is emphasized because they never consciously knew of this principle or what it was that literally swept them up the stairway to eminent success.

Source: *PMA Science of Success Course.* Pgs. 504 & 505.

Self-Definition
By Dr. James B. Hill

Dr. James B. Hill

Four years ago, I sat out there where you are today and listened to a man named Jim Amos. Mr. Amos made a fortune with "Mail Boxes, Inc." He sold his company to UPS for something upwards of 800 million dollars. He was a young man, maybe 55 or so. He was wildly successful!

But the day that he stood where I am standing today, Jim Amos did not talk about how he achieved success. He talked about self-definition. He said the day will come, whether we are successful or not, when we have to come to terms with who we are.

How do you define yourself?

Think about that for a second–Who are you?...

Are you a Napoleon Hill Scholar? A top student? Are you a successful businessman? A super athlete? A tenured professor? A noble laureate?

Aren't these just the things that we do?

If we define ourselves by what we do, how then do we define ourselves when we stop doing those things?

For much of my life, I was a Marine; I certainty thought of myself as one. I am just as proud today of being a Marine as I am of being a Doctor. But is that who I am? Do you look at me and "think" MARINE? Before that I was a merchant seaman. Is that who I am? People who know all of my history certainly don't think of me as a Marine...**or as a merchant seaman.**

I listened to Mr. Amos and realized that for all of my life I have been defining myself by how I made my living. And worse, I also defined others by what they did.

I remember feeling chills run up and down my spine as I wrestled with Mr. Amos' question? I could not answer it. It bothered me–a lot.

Who am I?

My Dream

That night I dreamed that I was standing in line before Peter at the gates to heaven, awaiting my judgment.

When my time came, I stepped up to Peter who was looking at his books. He looked up at me and snarled, "Who are you and why do you think you deserve to enter heaven?"

I answered, "Well, I am a doctor; I am not a bad guy; I help people, I...."

Peter slammed the book of atonement shut, interrupting

192

me to say, "I didn't ask you what you did for a living–did I?"

"Besides, you didn't really become a doctor just to help your fellow man, did you?...You just wanted to please your family! OR maybe you just wanted to irritate your X!" (Yes, this Peter was mean...I guess he was in a bad mood; **he had been sending people to Hell all day.**)

"I ask you again, WHO are you?"

I could not answer. I didn't know.

After telling me that it was clear that I didn't know the answer, Peter said he would send me back for a year to get one. He warned that I had better have an answer when I came before him again.

Well, I woke up after this incredible, indelible dream, feeling a bit shaken.

For the next year, I thought long and hard about Peter's question. I admit that I sweated a bit as Peter's deadline approached–remember, he gave me a year. I finally concluded that...

I...don't...know!

enough over [illegible] that [illegible] what would be a living [illegible]

Besides, you liked to have preachers about you to tell [illegible] and [illegible] you [illegible] please [illegible] feels [illegible] people [illegible] anyway [illegible] The [illegible] free, sending people to sleep all day.

[illegible]

[illegible]

[illegible] and [illegible] for a [illegible] came [illegible]

Well, I [illegible] and [illegible] be [illegible]

After the next year, it was not long and [illegible] question [illegible] experience [illegible] finally concluded that

[illegible]

GOOD ^{AS} GOLD
43

It is no more correct for a man to be defined by his job or his success than it is for him to be defined by his failure.

–Dr. J. B. Hill

A "can do" attitude positions us for success. We cannot succeed if we fail to try. Those who are afraid to try basically need to cultivate self-confidence. Without trust in yourself and confidence in your ability, you will never meet your basic expectations let alone exceed them.

Napoleon Hill's self-confidence formula is worth reading, displaying, and even memorizing. It is several auto-suggestions all rolled into one short essay and has proven its worth over time. Whether you read it silently, out loud, or recite it from memory, you are conditioning your subconscious mind for ultimate success. This strange technique always guarantees a positive outcome, but does not guarantee the time or the place when the outcome will occur. It fine tunes your receptors for success opportunities and creates a level of awareness that you may otherwise overlook. For example, let's say you are looking for income generating opportunities. Without boosting your self confidence, you may not recognize or even ignore a plan that is brought to your attention. But with this formula, when an opportunity arises your conscious mind is alerted to what your unconscious mind has been conditioned to discover.

In his definition of the conscious and the subconscious

minds, Dr. Hill states: "The conscious mind is the architect; the subconscious mind is the vast storehouse from which may be requisitioned the mental materials for the project which is under construction. The conscious mind makes the plan and decides what shall be done. The subconscious mind develops the power to do it."

In utilizing our standard equipment, the conscious and the subconscious minds work in tandem. But in order to fulfill your goals and dreams, you must first prime the pump, stoke the fire, visualize the outcome, engage your senses, and position yourself for success. That requires self-confidence and self-determination. You have to have a plan in order to work the plan. The plan is the map. The journey is a real life step-by-step process that enables you to cross the terrain and arrive at your destination one step at a time. You probably have heard the expression that success leaves footprints, right? It's true. When you emulate someone else's actions, good or bad, you arrive at the destination that they achieved. Think about it. "Would you like to swing on a star, carry moonbeams home in a jar, be better off than you are, or, would you rather be a pig?" You already know the routine for success and it all boils down to your greatest power–the power to choose. Choose wisely.

Self-Confidence Formula
by Napoleon Hill

I know that I have the ability to achieve the object of my definite purpose in life; therefore, I *demand* of myself persistent, continuous action toward its attainment, and I here and now promise to render such action.

I realize the dominating thoughts of my mind will eventually reproduce themselves in outward, physical action, and gradually transform themselves into physical reality; therefore, I will concentrate my thought, for thirty minutes daily, upon the task of thinking of the person I intend to become, thereby creating in my mind a clear mental picture.

I know through the principle of autosuggestion, any desire that I persistently hold in my mind will eventually seek expression through some practical means of attaining the object back of it; therefore, I will devote ten minutes daily to demanding of myself the development of *self-confidence.*

I have clearly written down a description of my *definite chief* aim in life, and I will never stop trying, until I shall have developed sufficient self-confidence for its attainment.

I fully realize that no wealth or position can long endure, unless built upon truth and justice; therefore, I will engage in no transaction that does not benefit all whom it affects. I will succeed by attracting to myself the forces I wish to use, and the cooperation of other people. I will induce others to serve me, because of my willingness to serve others. I will eliminate hatred, envy, jealousy, selfishness, and cynicism, by developing love for all humanity, because I know that a negative attitude toward others can never bring me success. I will cause others to believe in me, because I will believe in them, and in myself. I will sign my name to this formula, commit it to memory, and repeat it aloud once a day, with full faith that it will gradually influence my thoughts and actions so that I will become a self-reliant, and successful, person.

Back of this formula is a law of nature that no man has yet been able to explain. The name by which one calls this law is of little importance. The important fact about it is—it *works* for the glory and success of mankind, *if* it is used constructively. On the other hand, if used destructively, it will destroy just as readily. In this statement may be found a very significant truth, namely, that those who go down in defeat, and end their lives in poverty, misery, and distress, do so because of negative application of the principle of autosuggestion. The cause may be found in the fact that all impulses of thought have a tendency to clothe themselves in their physical equivalent.

Source: *Think and Grow Rich* by Napoleon Hill. Collector's Edition. Pgs. 86 & 87.

Self-Definition Part 2
By Dr. James B. Hill

Dr. James B. Hill

It is no more correct for a man to be defined by his job or his success than it is for him to be defined by his failure. Now, this does not mean that I failed to get an answer for Peter. I just don't know if it is correct.

I have come to believe that self-definition has to be in terms of the roles we play in human society.

Am I a good man, a good father, a good American? Do I use my skills and talents to help others?

These are the things by which others **who know us** will judge us and by which we must judge ourselves.

It is no more correct for a man to be defined by his job or his success than it is for him to be defined by his failure.

When next I appear before St. Peter and he asks me who I am...I know the answer that I will give...I will tell him simply...I am a good daddy.

I hope I am "good enough" because I have no doubt that the Peter in my dreams is going to check his book of atonement.

Abandoning your dreams is easy.

The second thing that I want to talk about today is sacrificing your dreams for success. A few years ago, I had dinner with a number of interesting, educated men and women.

Everyone at my table was familiar with Napoleon Hill and his philosophy. Discussion flowed freely as it does so well between people with similar and familiar viewpoints.

The table talk pertained to Napoleon Hill and his principles. We all nodded agreement when points were made.

All of a sudden I started to wonder if any of these successful people had ACTUALLY USED Napoleon Hill as a guide. So, I asked...

Silence descended. I had insulted them. Everyone (and I

do mean everyone) glared at me.

Finally, a man cleared his throat and said the obvious..." Well of course! It would have been impossible to achieve success without using it!"

After apologizing and assuring them that my insult was unintentional, I offered clarification by restating my question.

They had all achieved success but had they achieved their dreams?

Again there was silence but this time is was from introspection.

Nobody responded and I had my answer.

They were all successful and yet somehow they had all failed to achieve their dreams–goals, yes, but not their dreams.

Let me explain this with another story next week.

Introduction: Dr. J.B. Hill

When Dr. Hill was 12, his grandfather gave him $10, some advice, and an autographed copy of *"Think and Grow Rich,"* Napoleon Hill's influential book. He says he spent the money, ignored the advice and lost the book. However, he says his grandfather's book would later change his life.

Napoleon Hill was born in poverty in a one-room cabin on the Pound River on Oct. 26, 1883. From these humble beginnings, the Wise County native became an advisor to presidents and a best-selling author. During the early 20th century, Hill interviewed the nation's most successful business leaders, including Andrew Carnegie and Henry Ford. Hill compiled his eight-volume set *The Law of Success,* a collection of the philosophy of individual achievement. He later condensed his research to compile *Think and Grow Rich,* often called one of the most important motivational books ever written.

Dr. Hill, born in Morgantown, W.Va., is the son of David Hill, the youngest son of Napoleon Hill and Florence Hornor. He graduated from high school in 1966 and spent time in the Merchant Marines until 1969, when he was drafted into service as a private with the United States Marine Corps.

By 1973, he had been promoted five times to the rank of staff sergeant and given the opportunity to attend Vanderbilt University, where he spent 3 years earning a bachelor's degree in mechanical engineering. At graduation, he was commissioned as a second lieutenant and commenced service in the Marines as a field artillery officer. He later earned a master's degree in mathematics from the Naval Postgraduate School.

As an officer, he held command twice, led a team of military advisors into Southeast Asia, briefed the Soviet General Staff, served as aide-de-camp to two Marine Corps generals, taught mathematics at the U.S. Naval Academy, and served in many critical billets at the battery, battalion, and regimental level. He is certified in scuba, mountain, cold weather, and jungle warfare and is a graduate of the Army's Command and General Staff College.

In 1995, he retired from the Marine Corps after 26 years of service to study medicine. At the age of 53, he graduated from medical school and started a three-year residency in family medicine. Dr. Hill is now board-certified in family medicine and holds certifications in wound care and hyperbaric medicine.

GOOD AS GOLD
44

You will reflect upon your life some day to discover you cannot find your measure because you lost the opportunity to measure yourself against your dreams.

−Dr. J. B. Hill

In today's final segment from Dr. J. B. Hill, he discusses why deferred dreams are not always a good plan. When tradeoffs are made and goals downsized it often has the same effect as buying something that lacks quality. The item doesn't last as long as it should and it needs to be replaced sooner.

A real lifelong goal is based upon your authentic mission in life, and when you find out what this goal is, it takes a lifetime to accomplish it. In finding your authentic purpose, I once read that it is a product of both your personality and your spiritual self. Personally, I like that idea, because this combination can only come together because of who you are, and as a consequence you are the only person in the entire universe who can give your unique gift to the world. Therefore, everyone has something special to gift to the world, and it should not be deferred because if you never get around to it, this personalized gift will be lost forever.

Langston Hughes wrote a poem that I like on this subject. It reads as follows:

A Dream Deferred

What happens to a dream deferred?

Does it dry up
like a raisin in the sun?
Or fester like a sore—
And then run?
Does it stink like rotten meat?
Or crust and sugar over—
like a syrupy sweet?

Maybe it just sags
like a heavy load.

Or does it explode?

In reading this poem, it seems as if all the consequences of deferring our dreams are not good ones. Just as Dr. J. B. Hill cautions Scott, sometimes dreams are hard to recapture. It's best not to quit when the going gets tough. Rather, as we all have heard the better approach is that the tough get going. How can we master our dreams if we can't discipline ourselves? In this one instance I believe that Napoleon Hill would agree that the word "impossible" applies. So, get tough and be all you can be! Each one of us has a treasure waiting to be given away. Don't defer making the gift.

Self-Discipline
by Napoleon Hill

Self-discipline begins with the mastery of your thoughts. If you do not control your thoughts, you cannot control your deeds. Therefore, in its simplest form, self-discipline causes you to think first and act afterward. Almost everyone automatically does exactly the reverse of this. People generally act first and think later—unless they take possession of their minds and control their thoughts and deeds through self-discipline.

Control of the Emotions

Self-discipline will give you complete control over fourteen major emotions listed below. Seven of these are positive, and seven negative:

Positive Emotions	Negative Emotions
Love	Fear
Sex	Jealousy
Hope	Hatred
Faith	Revenge
Enthusiasm	Greed
Loyalty	Anger
Desire	Superstition

All of these emotions are states of mind and are, therefore, subject to your control and direction. You can see instantly how dangerous the seven negative emotions can be if they are not mastered. The seven positive emotions can be destructive too, if they are not organized and released under your complete, conscious control. Wrapped up in these fourteen emotions is power of a truly explosive nature. If you regulate it properly, it can lift you to heights of distinguished achievement. But if you permit it to run rampant, it can dash you to pieces on the rocks of failure. You should realize that your education, your experience, your native intelligence and your good intentions cannot alter or modify these possibilities.

Source: *PMA Science of Success Course.* Pgs. 268 & 269.

Self-Definition Part 3
By Dr. James B. Hill

Dr. James B. Hill

"You will know that you have forgotten your dreams when you find yourself waiting for something to happen."

Scott, the son of a close friend of mine, resigned from the Naval Academy during his plebe year after spending 8 months there.

One evening over dinner, he told me that he planned to attend Georgia Tech in the fall.

He then surprised me by saying that he could return to the Academy the following year but he would have to repeat the entire plebe year.

Scott asked me for my thoughts. After asking his Dad if I could speak freely, I told Scott....

That I could see him graduating from Georgia Tech with a fine engineering degree. I saw him getting a great job, marrying a pretty girl, having great kids, and leading a life of convenience, comfort and security. A success by any measure!

However, I went on to say, "Scott, do you remember the talks we had before you went to the Naval Academy? About what it could mean to be an academy graduate?

"You talked about commanding an aircraft carrier, flying an F-18 fighter plane, and maybe walking on the moon. You wondered what it would be like to dive in the Sea of Japan or to have an opportunity to lead Marines.

"Scott, If you do not return to the academy, you will never command an aircraft carrier and you will never walk on the moon or fly an F-18. You will never dive in the Sea of Japan and you will never have a chance to lead Marines.

"Candidly, Scott, I believe you will regret a decision not to return to the academy for the rest of your life.

"You will reflect upon your life some day to discover you cannot find your measure <u>because you lost the opportunity to measure yourself</u> against your dreams."

Lost Dreams

I think this happens to many successful people. We trade our dreams for good jobs and the security that success brings to each of us.

This is what happened to those people I talked about earlier. They were successful by any measure. They knew and had put to practice much of Napoleon Hill's philosophy with good results. Nevertheless, they had been blindsided by success and had lost the vision to achieve their dreams.

Someday, they are likely to look back at successful and meaningful lives and, as with those who have failed, may whisper...

"I could-dah been a contender!"

"I could-dah!"

A Solution

There is a reason, of course, why this happens to so many people—they lose their focus.

Napoleon Hill explained how to stay focused by using the power of the sub-conscious mind. <u>He wrote that we could enlist this power by thought</u> and suggested that we write our goals down to read and ponder twice a day.

Theologians suggest this as well. To strengthen faith and commitment, they tell us to <u>reconcile daily through prayer in which we assess where we are spiritually.</u> Did we sin today and if we did, have we atoned for it by doing something good?

But however you do it, remember your dreams.

You will know that you have forgotten your dreams when you find yourself waiting for something to happen.

When you realize you are waiting for something to happen, it is time for you to remember your dream and to remember that you are the only one that can make it happen.

Closing

As you continue to achieve success after success, remember: Avoid defining yourself by that success and . . . Never forget your dreams!

GOOD ^{AS} GOLD
45

When we incorporate Thanksgiving into our everyday life we begin a cycle of gratitude that in turn will prove to be a force in our life that will attract countless meaningful experiences along the journey to our dreams.

–Raven Blair Davis

Recently I vacationed in Europe and encountered "worry beads." I had purchased some years ago and found the ritual of using these beads as a mechanism for reducing stress and worry interesting. This time when I saw them, I asked myself why these beads could not be renamed gratitude beads? It makes far more sense to count your blessings and focus on giving thanks than it does to count your worries and focus on your problems. Also, traveling recently to Jamaica and hearing that in Jamaica that there are "no problems" only "situations," it made me recall the idea that truly what we think about we become. We can color our mind to be positive or to be negative, and the choice is always ours. If we say we have a problem, we do. If we identify the problem as a situation, immediately the focus becomes less negative. "No problem" can ease you out of a negative mental attitude just because you choose to acknowledge the situation and not the problem. Redefine your problems as situations and see if you worry less. All it takes is a change in your vocabulary for a more positive outlook on life.

A good "thanks giving" exercise for young and old alike is to make a long list of all the things you are grateful for–and here's a sampling of mine to get you started!

I am grateful for:
1) My cat's purr as he greets me after an absence
2) The taste of raspberries in or out of season
3) The warmth of my electric blanket on the preheat cycle
4) The smell of burning leaves in autumn in the Midwest
5) A handwritten note from a friend nearby or far away
6) My own bed after traveling away from home
7) Visiting my sisters' homes in Florida and seeing things through their eyes
8) A candle burning in the morning on my kitchen table as I write in my journal
9) The scent of pine swags on the door for the holidays
10) Finding my choice of a novel to read for leisure at the thrift store
11) Receiving emails from family, friends, and international acquaintances
12) An unexpected gift that arrives in the mail or on my doorstep

Well, you get the idea. Now, rather than counting your worries, or counting sheep, why not begin right now to count your favorite things? How can you not feel better after listing what you enjoy most about life? Nothing is required except pure appreciation for what you have been gifted by the Universe. Look, really look, and you will be amazed at what you take for granted.

Start with each of the senses. Ask yourself what you enjoy that you can see, hear, taste, smell or touch? Pretend you are without a sense. What would you miss if you lost, say, your hearing? As you will begin to realize, we do take so much for granted. Being reminded to be thankful one day a year is not sufficient. Daily we need to wake up with gratitude on our mind, and a desire to recite an extended "thank you" to the Universe for all we have received. If you practice this, you will be amazed how your outlook colors your world. And with that, you are practicing the true spirit of thanks giving with one amazing thank you after another for all the gifts you have received in your lifetime. Happy Thanks Giving!

Willingness to Share One's Blessings
by Napoleon Hill

He who has not learned the blessed art of sharing has not learned the true path of happiness, for happiness comes only by sharing. And let it be forever remembered that all riches may be embellished and multiplied by the simple process of sharing them where they may serve others. And let it be also remembered that the space one occupies in the hearts of his fellowmen is determined precisely by the service he renders through some form of sharing his blessings.

Riches which are not shared, whether they be material riches or the intangibles, wither and die like the rose on a severed stem, for it is one of Nature's first laws that inaction and disuse lead to decay and death, and this law applies to the material possessions of men just as it applies to the living cells of every physical body.

Source: *The Master-Key to Riches.* Fawcett Crest Book. 1965, Pg. 22.

Creed for Riches
by Napoleon Hill

I give thanks daily, not for mere riches, but for wisdom with which to recognize, embrace, and properly use the great abundance of riches I now have at my command. I have no enemies because I injure no man for any cause, but I try to benefit all with whom I come in contact, by teaching them the way to enduring riches. I have more material wealth than I need because I am free from greed and covet only the material things I can use while I live.

Source: *PMA Science of Success Course.* Pg. 25

GOOD AS GOLD
46

People want to be of service to others. People want to help one another, give back to their community, help others discover the principles of Dr. Napoleon Hill, help others discover a way to earn extra ongoing income streams to help better support their families, help groups and charities who need to raise much needed funds find a simple way to contribute to their worthwhile causes, and help others feel good!

—Shane Morand

Oftentimes the news can be depressing. Daily we see situation after situation of man's inhumanity to man. Stories revolving around hatred, misuse of power, lack of trustworthiness, murders and mayhem—all on the evening news. When a person watches this daily, how can one not become depressed and assume that the world is not a safe and positive place? Even though the average person would prefer to make a positive difference, it seems like an unattainable task in a world that has gone haywire.

In order to create peace and harmony in both our outer and inner worlds, we must first become peaceful ourselves. We begin by thinking peaceful thoughts and next following up with peaceful actions. Getting into the pattern of doing this is not as easy as it seems. There is a price to be paid, and that price is self-discipline. First we must train ourselves in a positive way to become peace-keeping citizens of the world, and then model this behavior for all to see. Being reactionary seems to come naturally, but being peaceful and positive takes more self-control. Flying off the handle is easier than quietly reflecting on our response first, but the outcome can make an immense difference.

Isn't it time to take control of the world's situation by performing deeds related to goodness rather than evil? Evil makes the news, but goodness is the true path toward ultimate success. The price to be paid involves a personal commitment from each and every world citizen and it involves our greatest power–the power to choose right from wrong. Abraham Lincoln stated that he lived a simple philosophy. When he did good, he consequently felt good. And, when he did the opposite, he did not feel good regarding his actions. Isn't this essentially true for each of us? Why then do we not pursue good and shun the bad? Possibly because the personal gratification can be delayed, possibly because there is no overt reward, possibly because it is not the popular choice to make, and just possibly because we just don't know any better.

How do we proceed? We advance by taking one single positive step at a time. Try asking yourself the simple question, "What should I do next to make the world a better place?" Then listen to that still, small voice within that gives you direction as to what to do. I bet it doesn't tell you to capitalize on someone's misfortune, or to reduce someone's self-confidence by not acknowledging their gradual improvement. Change takes time. It does not happen overnight. But, if we are to move in a positive direction we must begin by recognizing that there is a positive and a negative choice. If we want to improve our world for ourselves and others, the world won't begin to show improvement until we begin right now, today, right where we are to do something overtly positive for the betterment of someone else. Reciprocity makes the world harmonize. Do something today that jumpstarts harmony rather than hatred. And, do not look for the reward–it will arrive right on time where you least expect to find it–in your own backyard.

Why Create Enthusiasm?
by Napoleon Hill

Enthusiasm is literally the gateway of approach to your spiritual qualities. It not only gives deep conviction to the words you speak, but it projects its influence into the inner recesses of the soul of anyone whom it touches.

Enthusiasm is a builder of new ideas.

It is not surprising, therefore, that Ralph Waldo Emerson said: *"Nothing great was ever achieved without enthusiasm."* For he had felt the rebound of enthusiasm in his own soul, where it revealed to him the hidden forces of his being and made his name immortal.

And it was this same rebound of enthusiasm, deep within the soul of Helen Keller, which inspired her with the faith through which she mastered her afflictions of deafness, dumbness and blindness.

It carried Edison through ten thousand failures and revealed to him, at long last, the secret of the incandescent electric lamp. Psychologists who have studied Edison's achievements all agree that his astounding physical endurance was inspired by his enduring enthusiasm for his definite major purpose.

It was this same undying enthusiasm for the cause of American Independence which inspired George Washington to keep on fighting in the face of seemingly insurmountable obstacles until freedom and liberty had been secured for the United States of America.

And it was the power of enthusiasm which inspired the people of the United States to awaken, prepare and take action to meet another great emergency which threatened their freedom and safety at the outbreak of World War II–an achievement which astounded the world because of the efficiency and dispatch with which it was carried out.

Enthusiasm was the power which sustained Abraham Lincoln during the Civil War and enabled him to carry on until he had saved the nation from self-destruction.

"How," you may ask, "can power be attained?"

The procedure is simple and within the control of everyone, as the Creator intended it should be:

You start with hope–hope for the achievement of some definite purpose.

Hope is the forerunner of faith.

And the smoldering embers of hope are fanned into the white flame of faith by feeding them on controlled enthusiasm backed by definiteness of purpose. The fanning process should be continued until ordinary desire becomes burning desire.

Hope, enthusiasm, and faith are the key words because of their close relationship. When they are combined with definiteness of purpose, they give one access to unlimited mind-power. These are the four factors which lead to a burning desire.

Hope alone is of little value. It is but little more than a wish, and everyone has wishes in abundance. Nothing comes of wishes until they are organized and associated with their companions: definiteness of purpose, enthusiasm and faith.

The process of organization takes place through self-discipline. This is the principle through which enthusiasm may be organized, controlled and directed to a definite end. Other principles of this philosophy which are related to enthusiasm and which may be needed for its organization and control are:

Definiteness of Purpose

The Master Mind

Pleasing Personality

Personal Initiative

The Habit of Learning from Defeat

The Habit of Going the Extra Mile

Applied Faith

Creative Vision

Concentration

The Habit of Health

Accurate Thinking

214

Mastery and application of these twelve principles will place you within easy reach of controlled enthusiasm. This has been the experience of every person who has mastered this philosophy, and it will be yours!

Men of great achievement are men of great desires. You will have such desires, and achieve them, if you will follow the instructions you have been given. Remember: Anything in life worth having is worth working for. And there is a price to be paid. The price for reaping the benefits of this philosophy consists mainly in eternal vigilance and everlasting persistence in applying such a philosophy as a daily habit. Mere knowledge is not enough. It must be applied.

Enthusiasm is a combination of mental and physical energy which is seldom found in an ailing body. It thrives best where sound physical health abounds. Sound health begins with the development and maintenance of health consciousness, just as economic success begins with prosperity consciousness.

Source: *PMA Science of Success Course*: Pgs. 261, 262 & 263.

GOOD AS GOLD
47

The rich are willing to take risks that the non-rich are not. The non-rich want to play it safe, but hit it big. It doesn't work that way. To hit it big you need to take big risks . . . the rewards are commensurate with the risk.

–Madeleine Kay

Ever hear of the term "group think"? It is said to occur when a pervasive mindset becomes the dominating thought pattern for a group such as a nation, culture, organization, family, or any other group of like-minded individuals. Take a moment and consider whether or not you subscribe to "group think" on a small or large basis, and then consider the consequences of abdicating your right of free will in making your own decisions. At times it can be easy and beneficial to go with the flow of existing thought, but at other times it can be equally detrimental and imprison one in outdated methods of thinking that create your daily life and destiny–much like a self-fulfilling prophecy.

For example, if one accepts the notion that wealth is unattainable because of the income level of your birth family, a "group think" pattern is in place that resembles a cookie cutter. When your dough is spread out on the table, and the only cookie cutter in your baking drawer is a pine tree, all your cookies will be in the shape of that evergreen. But, if you envision shapes such as angels, stars, and bells, you can potentially expand your creativity and carve out equally beautiful, yet different cookies. Ultimately, the choice is yours.

Likewise with the creation of wealth and financial fortune, you can follow the tried and true and get what you've always got or stray from the beaten path and try something new. "New" could be formal education, accredited training, travel, an investment, a calculated risk, or a creative idea put into action. All it takes is one good plan that is followed up with measurable, observable action steps. And, if that plan turns out poorly, then all that is required for eventual success is a refinement of the plan, not a new goal.

Has someone told you it couldn't be done? Have you questioned their basis of authority? Or, have you joined their group? Why not start today by questioning some of your strongly held beliefs? Beliefs are comfort zones. Comfort zones can be like warm fuzzy housecoats or straight jackets. Make sure you recognize which one you are wearing. Direct your thoughts, control your emotions, and ordain your destiny.

Wealth Creates Wealth
by Napoleon Hill

Wealth creates wealth. A large sum of money in the hands of one man generally does not create as much wealth as does money which circulates, provided that those who handle its circulation are interested in creating wealth.

A man's happiness and peace of mind depend on his sharing all kinds of wealth. Business relations cannot properly be described as a relationship of love between buyer and seller; yet when the idea of service to one's fellow men comes into the relationship, much that is profitable to both parties also enters in. "A little bit of myself," said Henry Ford, "goes into every automobile that rolls off our assembly lines, and I think of every automobile we sell, not in terms of the profit it yields us, but in terms of the useful service it may render the purchaser." Thomas A. Edison said: "I never perfected an invention that I did not think about in terms of the service it might give others."

The idea that a business should give its customers more

than a product for a price is not new, and history proves it creates both good businesses and good customers. Good relations between an industrial employer and his employees, however, are not very old as history goes. This is natural enough when we consider that enterprises which employ people by the thousand have not been with us more than a few generations. They are a great way for the owner of the business to make money, and unfortunately many a labor force has been badly treated in the process.

In past years we have our own era of those industrial pirates who never thought of sharing with their employees the wealth their employees helped to create. While they made a great show of their money in New York, Newport or Palm Beach those men would have sneered at the idea that a society needs a large number of well-paid people who are able to buy more goods and lead better lives.

Millionaires are far more numerous today. More than five thousand new millionaires have so declared themselves on their tax returns in the last decade. Also, as I have mentioned, today's millionaires do not seem to want the notice that rich men used to require. Most of my readers will not recognize the names of some of the present-day millionaires and multimillionaires I have cited.

Nor do today's moneyed men seem anxious to form a definite class to which the poor may not aspire. I quote Arthur Decio, who made so much money in building and selling mobile homes: "It's easier to get ahead than it was fifteen or forty years ago. Look at the population growth and the tremendous rise in personal income. . .This country is just loaded with opportunities."

So it is, and many of the opportunities would not exist if wealth were not better distributed than it used to be. Employers have seen the value to themselves, to their people and to society of taking workers into partnership with industry. A capitalist society proves over and over that it is the best way to create maximum, widespread wealth.

Source: *Grow Rich! With Peace of Mind*. 1967. Fawcett Crest. Pgs. 80 & 81.

GOOD ^{AS} GOLD
48

You can have all the technical expertise in the world, but if you can't get in front of well-qualified prospects and then be able to influence them to do business with you, you'll wind up as one of the 90% of business casualties.

–Jim Rohrbach

What is that special something that causes one person to be a success and another to miss the mark? In Dr. Hill's analysis of over 500 men who hit the bull's eye of financial success, he surmised that both initiative and persistence were key factors that were essential ingredients in the wealth formula. Funny, but many people today do not believe that success is that hard or that work intensive. False belief in the exclusive power of the subconscious mind leads many to think that success is just a thought away—maybe an intensely visualized thought, but still a thought. Dr. Hill explicitly states that "thoughts are things," but he is definitive in his next remarks when he states that these thoughts must be followed by action. Trouble is, many aspiring to success do not know which actions to take. How does one acquire direction when he or she is lacking an internal success compass? Two actions to be put into practice are personal initiative and persistence. Without drive and a performance ethic, little will be accomplished. But, when a person conditions himself to take action regularly, the doing aids in creating the desire to do more. It becomes a habit, and this habit creates the desire–almost a compulsion–to advance one step at a time in the direction of one's choosing.

Consider for a moment those individuals who dream or wish for a better life. What action steps do they take to make this a reality? Do they seek out opportunities to market their ideas or their services, or do they wait for someone to knock on their door? Just by taking the initial step of writing down your definite major purpose and the timeline for its attainment, you are moving out of the dream state into the action state. Next, you begin step by step in working the plan you outlined by taking consistent movement toward your objective. It really doesn't matter what it is. It just matters that it resonates with you and does not harm another human being. That provides a large choice of opportunities that you can pursue.

If making a choice of purpose and plan is a difficult choice now, why not emulate a plan already in place? Oftentimes plans are created by others that you decide to follow. A high school diploma, a college degree, a marriage contract, vows in a religious community, are all plans that people agree to in order to fulfill a need, reach an objective, create a life plan, etc., and they were outlined by others. Practice first. If you consider yourself an "average" person who hasn't yet achieved a great deal, you'll need to start small by working on something simple first. And then "graduate" to the big stuff. The truth is you will not hit a home run on the first pitch–you begin by learning how to get on first base.

Review plans that you have fulfilled already in your life. Consider the part personal initiative and persistence played in helping you reach your goal. Once you understand the map, the actual territory should not be hard to traverse. You can achieve any goal that you set for yourself through personal initiative and followed through with persistence. These are the ingredients that dreams are made of–why not try them out for yourself? You are only rubbing shoulders with success when you take continuous, persistent action fueled by your own personal initiative for the attainment of your definite major purpose.

Road to Success
by Napoleon Hill

From today on you should take advantage of the opportunities that come to the person who uses initiative, because this is one of the most important sign boards on the Road to Success.

Your instructions in connection with this sign board on Initiative are simple and easily followed. For the next ten days make it your business to use Initiative by doing at least one thing each day that you are not told to do in connection with your work. Say nothing to anyone about what you are doing, but keep your own counsel and follow these instructions. If your work is of such a nature that you cannot perform work that you are not told to perform, then speed up a bit and perform more work and better work than you have been performing in the same length of time. Keep this up for ten days and by that time you will attract attention of your employer. You will also see, by the end of the ten days, that it will pay you to use Initiative the remainder of your life, because Initiative leads to greater responsibility, to a bigger pay envelope and helps you to get whatever you have decided upon as your definite aim in life.

Source: *Napoleon Hill's Magazine.* November, 1922. Pg. 30.

GOOD AS GOLD
49

I visited Napoleon's friends too–Carnegie, Edison, Morgan, Schwab–the whole lot of them. I knew them all. And you know what–they knew me too. They believed in me because they were visionaries. They knew that a belief in me was part of their training for a lifetime of service. Their burning desire for a red wagon or a new pair of shoes from me back in the day was what fueled them to develop more significant desires later in life.

–Santa Claus

Today is Christmas Day. And, the real magic is inside each of us. The Christmas Magic, that is. Our thoughts create the magical outcomes in our lives. Sometimes we forget that our source is always internal. Nothing external can make us happy for long. It's truly the recognition that gifts from the heart are really the best gifts of all. If you have forgotten these gifts on your list this year, there is still time today to present a few to those who are your nearest and dearest. Always make sure that you attach the "heart"strings. They are the very best ribbons of all.

Below are 52 priceless quotations from Dr. Napoleon Hill that will fill your stocking all year long. Many can be used as affirmations, as daily thought starters, as notes to a friend, or as expressions of gratitude to the Universe for all the good you receive daily. Feel free to pass them along too. I am certain that they will be cherished in the recipient's heart for many Christmases to come–no strings attached.

Napoleon Hill's
Positive Mental Attitude Stocking Stuffers

A good teacher is always a good student. - NH

A positive mind finds a way it can be done. A negative mind looks for all the ways it can't be done. - NH

All big things are made of smaller things of a related nature. - NH

As long as you are willing to let life push you around, it will. - NH

Close the door of fear behind you, and see how quickly the door to success opens in front of you. - NH

Create a definite plan for carrying out your desire and begin at once, whether you are ready or not, to put this plan into action. - NH

Courtesy is not dependent on education, but on common sense. - NH

Decisions without actions are worthless. - NH

Do it now . . . and before anyone tells you to do it! - NH

Do not settle for anything short of what you want. - NH

Don't look to the stars for the cause of your misfortunes. Look to yourself and get better results. - NH

Drifting through life without aim or purpose is the first cause of failure. - NH

Great achievement is born out of struggle. - NH

Happiness is found in doing, not merely in possessing. - NH

Happiness may be found only by helping others to find it. - NH

If I had one wish that would be granted for the asking, I would ask for more wisdom. - NH

If you don't know what you want from life, what do you think you'll get? - NH

If you set a goal, you are more apt to recognize things that will help you achieve it than if you don't set a goal. - NH

If you're unhappy with your world and want to change it, the place to begin is with yourself. - NH

It is better to imitate a successful man than to envy him. - NH

It is not necessary for others to fail in order that you may succeed. - NH

It's helpful to know that you move toward and become that which you think about. - NH

Keep your mind on the things you want and off the things you don't want. - NH

Meet the most important living person! That person is you. - NH

More gold has been mined from the brains of men than has ever been taken from the earth. - NH

No man can achieve greatness alone. - NH

No man can become a permanent success without taking others along with him. - NH

No two minds ever come together without creating a third invisible force, which may be likened to a "third mind." - NH

One little word—"please"—carries the power of great charm. - NH

Remember to express gratitude every day—by prayer and affirmation—for the blessings you have. - NH

Some nuggets of thought are worth more than nuggets of gold. - NH

Some people have learned to use the winds of adversity to sail their ship of life. - NH

Sometimes it is wiser to join forces with an opponent that it is to fight. - NH

Speed and skill come from repetition of effort. - NH

Spoken words leave impressions. Printed words leave tracks. - NH

Success attracts success and failure attracts failure. - NH

Successful people keep their mind fixed on what they want - not on what they don't want. - NH

That which you think today becomes that which you are tomorrow. - NH

The imagination is the workshop of the soul where all the plans for individual achievement are shaped. - NH

The mind grows only through use; it atrophies through idleness. - NH

The more you discipline yourself, the less you will be disciplined by others. - NH

The most important ingredient of success is belief in yourself. - NH

The one thing nature will not tolerate is idleness! - NH

The power of thought is the only thing over which any human being has complete, unquestionable control. - NH

The secret to getting things done is to act. - NH

There is power in the spoken word...avoid all-inclusive, restrictive words such as never, only, nothing, every, everyone, no one and can't. - NH

Trying to get without giving is as fruitless as trying to reap without sowing. - NH

Whatever the mind can conceive and believe, the mind can achieve. - NH

You can do it if you believe you can. - NH

Your mind attracts what it dwells on—so keep your mind on the things you want and off the things you don't want. - NH

Your only real limitations are those you set up in your own mind. - NH

Your reputation is made by others. Your character is made by you. - NH

Your success or failure is in your own mind. - NH

Give Yourself A Christmas Present
by Napoleon Hill

May I suggest that this Christmas you can give yourself a present which will bring you riches in abundance, peace of mind, and attract to you enduring friendships?

The present I have in mind is something which only you

can give yourself, and it happens to be the only thing over which you have complete control.

It can change your entire life so completely that every circumstance you experience–every transaction you have with others–will bring you definite benefits.

It can help you transmute sorrow and adversity into powerful spiritual qualities which may add new strength to your religion, in times of emergency.

It can banish all forms of fear and substitute faith with which you can direct your activities to ends of your own choice.

This gift is so miraculous that it will extend to the lives of your loved ones and make them richer in the values which count for most in life.

It will attract to you new and unexpected opportunities for advancement in your occupation.

And it can rekindle the fires of love and friendship where they may have grown cold by neglect.

It can remove the causes of many physical ailments and help you enjoy a dynamic, healthful physical body.

It can give you the magic power to convert enemies into friends.

It can put something into your handshake which was not there before and give your spoken words forcefulness that will command respect and attention from others.

It can give you the alertness of mind with which to make definite and accurate decisions.

There is no substitute for this gift which only you can present to yourself.

It's name is a positive mental attitude.

It costs nothing except the will to appropriate it; however, the only way you can keep it is to give it first position through usage in the habits which control your daily living.

Source: *Success Unlimited.* December 1954, Pgs. 10 & 11.

G͟OOD ᴬˢ G͟OLD
50

We are afraid to leave our job, to go back to school,
to step out of our comfort zones. We live half a life!
That, my friends, is not Thinking and Growing Rich!
—**Marcus Paton**

Ever wish that you could rev up your energy? Do twice as much in half the time? Open doors where they were nailed shut before? Transmute failure into success? Seems like a pipe dream, doesn't it? Well, Napoleon Hill tells us that all we have to do is to think it, believe it, and then achieve it. Sounds super-simple, but the reality is that we have to be very cautious about what we petition the Universe for because as sure as the sun rises in the East we will receive that which we desire most in life. Fantasies become realities when we put energy behind them. The outcome is determined by the amount of action we put into the fantasy. Energy can become matter. Each and every one of us is living proof of that.

Today is New Year's Day. What plans have you outlined for your projects this coming year? Are you considering all aspects of your personality when you build your goals? We are multifaceted beings who are composed of physical, spiritual, social, emotional, financial, and mental components. It makes sense to address each of these parts when planning our goal sheet for the coming year. If you leave out an essential aspect of yourself, you will become more and more lopsided as you limp toward your goals.

A wheel won't roll well if a spoke or hub is damaged. If

you take care of the basic mechanisms in life, the outcomes will be smoother. We all know the sensation of being in a car with a slowly deflating tire. At first it is a bumpy ride but before we know it we reach a permanent standstill until the tire is changed. Why put yourself through the flat tire syndrome in 2010? Keep your wheel of life well-rounded and your trip will be almost effortless.

I wish you the very best on this New Year's Day. May your path of life be smooth and wide open, and may your travels be memorable and lead you to the best possible destination. As you fulfill your goals, remember to reach back and extend a hand to the person who needs a little help from one who has already made it!

Keep Your Mind Free
by Napoleon Hill

An open mind is a free mind.

The person who closes his mind to new ideas, concepts and people is locking a door that enslaves his own mentality. Intolerance is a two-edged scythe that on its backswing cuts off opportunities and lines of communication. When you open your mind, you give your imagination freedom to act for you.

It's hard to realize now that less than six decades ago there were men who laughed at the Wright Brothers' experiments at flight. And barely three decades ago, Lindbergh could scarcely find backers for his trans-Atlantic flight. Today, men of vision freely predict man will soon fly to the moon–but no one's laughing. It's the scoffers who are held in scorn.

A closed mind is a sign of a static personality. It lets progress pass it by and hence can never take advantage of the opportunities progress offers.

Only if you have an open mind can you grasp the full impact of the first rule of the science of success: "Whatever the mind of man can conceive and believe, the mind can achieve."

It would be well for you to take stock of yourself. Are you among those who say "I can" and "It will be done" or do you fall in the group that says "Nobody can"–at the very moment somebody else is accomplishing it? An open mind requires faith–in yourself, your fellow man and the Creator who laid out a pattern of progress for Man and his universe.

The days of superstition are gone. But the shadow of prejudice is as dark as ever. You can come out into the light by closely examining your own personality. Do you make decisions based on reason and logic rather than on emotion and preconceived ideas? Do you listen closely, attentively and thoughtfully to the other fellow's arguments? Do you seek for facts rather than hearsay and rumor?

The human mentality withers unless in constant contact with the stimulating influence of fresh thought. The Communists, in their brain-washing technique, know that the quickest way to break a man's will is to isolate his mind, cutting him off from books, newspapers, radio and other normal channels of intellectual communication.

Under such circumstances, the intellect dies for lack of nourishment. Only the strongest will and the purest faith can save it.

Is it possible that you have imprisoned your mind in a social and cultural concentration camp? Have you subjected yourself to a brain-washing of your own making, isolating you from ideas that could lead to success? If so, it's time to sweep aside the bars of prejudice that imprison your intellect.

Open your mind and set it free!

Source: *Success Unlimited.* December, 1960. Pg. 39.

GOOD AS GOLD
51

There is one key principle that he was not recognizing and applying: Personal Success Precedes Business Success!

—Kip Kint

Finding our true calling in life is usually not an easy task. Many of us try on different hats as we experiment with our life's vocation, or personal calling. Sometimes, we begin to close in on what gives our life true purpose only to back away when we become frightened or concerned that we are unable to make a living at what we like to do.

What we like to do or enjoy doing is usually what we are good at, and herein is our buried treasure: our calling or life's work. It does not benefit someone to pursue a career in an area that only provides them financial security without joy. Better to pursue a career that is short on finances but long on personal satisfaction. If you feel drawn to what you are doing, would do it for no monetary compensation whatsoever, are not compelled to watch the clock while you are doing it, and it harms no other living person, then you have found your calling or your talent.

Hidden assets are those traits that are sometimes buried within us and do not surface until a very real need calls them forth. It could be an adversity, a sense of dissatisfaction, or just the desire to do more that calls our greatest talents forward into our daily lives.

When these talents surface in our daily reality and are recognized by us, it is often like a homecoming because we have begun the journey within to our true self. Let the "constructive discontentment" that Dr. Hill discusses in the essay below lead you to discover the wealth that is inside you–your personal treasure chest!

Using Your Hidden Assets
by Napoleon Hill

Each of us has locked within us all that is necessary to achieve wealth and greatness. It's merely a matter of learning to use these hidden assets, of investing them so to speak, so we can cash in on them.

The tragic thing is that so many go through life without ever putting them to use. Sometimes, trouble and adversity is necessary to make people use their resourcefulness and brain power to achieve success.

A bookkeeper lost his job as Christmas was approaching. He had no money to buy his 10-year-old son a gift. Instead of merely despairing, he went to work making the boy a gift.

Using two wheels from a discarded baby carriage, a few pieces of lumber from the basement, and some bright red paint, he constructed a toy that captured the attention of the entire neighborhood.

Other children wanted similar toys. The demand grew so fast that the unemployed bookkeeper turned his basement into a factory, then moved his production to a real industrial plant.

The toy the bookkeeper designed was called the "scooter."

Or consider the case of a soldier returned from World War I. He had been a salesman before the war but was now unemployed. He used his hidden assets too. He took a chunk of ice cream, stuck a stick in it for a handle, dipped it in chocolate covering–and the Eskimo Pie was born!

Then there was a young man working as a filling station helper in Dallas. The work was hard, hours long, pay short– all adding up to a state of mind I call "constructive discontentment."

The young man began selling for a publisher of children's books. But instead of approaching parents, he made friends with school teachers and got their permission to tell the children in class about his books.

Then he would ask the children to arrange an appointment with their parents so he could sell them the books. The plan worked wonderfully and the last time I saw the young man he was preparing to go into the publishing business for himself.

Have you searched carefully for any "hidden" resources you've overlooked simply because they weren't in some form you could bank immediately?

Have you some plan or idea which might prove of great value if you brought it into the open and put it to use?

A very successful man once gave this splendid formula for gaining wealth.

"Get some useful item that will bring repeat sales," said he. "Then put everything you have into taking it to the millions of people who need it."

His name was F. W. Woolworth. He didn't create anything new. He merely took something old and gave it a new method of sales distribution.

The opportunities our country offers today are greater than ever—and growing constantly. Think, for example, of the millions to be made by someone who devises some simple method of reducing traffic accidents.

Somewhere you have unused assets. Put them to work for you and make yourself financially independent.

Source: *Success Unlimited.* December 1966, Pgs. 33 & 34.

GOOD ^{AS} GOLD
52

When we develop laser-like focus on our goals our minds are only focused on that which is necessary to accomplish those goals and then our minds start to notice "things that were not there before."
—Michael Wilkie

Self-discipline closes the door against jealousy, hatred, revenge, greed, anger and superstition, and opens the door to friendship, goodwill, confidence and love.
–Napoleon Hill

Most likely we have all heard the term "tough love." It is a technique wherein reality encounters fantasy head on and is intended to jerk the recipient back to the here and now for their own good. When parents apply this practice it frequently involves saying "no" or withholding some requested item such as money, a car, a down payment, or anything that the son or daughter is requesting that, in the minds of the parents, will not contribute in a positive way to the general good of the child.

Children grow up, parents die, and soon we realize that we are in their position and sometimes we find ourselves saying "no" to our own inner child. Maturity comes about through positive growth and frequently each of us can get in our own way. When we reach a developmental crossroads, we often prefer to take the traditional path and not put ourselves through extra work. Saying "yes" to the mundane can have its consequences too, because sooner rather than later we find that our path does not lead to growth but to stagnation. Napoleon Hill supplies the antidote to this illness of attitude, and it is called self-discipline.

Each of us is gifted with a conscience that generally works pretty well and provides good advice if we use it. Still, we often allow ourselves to linger in regret over past occurrences, mistakes, losses, and the like rather than positioning ourselves face forward toward a better future. Using the metaphor of door closing, Dr. Hill indicates that by closing the door tightly on our past, and not lingering in the threshold, we can move forward toward our life's purpose. This is not to say that we become hard-hearted or without compassion, but rather that we apply tough love to ourselves and care about who we are as much as we care about others.

Today, ask yourself if there is a door you have left ajar. Are you afraid to slam it shut and lock it and throw away the key? Consider that this option for retreat could be the reason that you are not moving forward. You are allowing a former setback to prevent your glorious comeback. Close that door now, and linger no further. New doors await you, and when you knock the doors will open and lead you to your destiny. Why wait? Make all things new.

Door Closing
by Napoleon Hill

Consider the rather serious problems which arise in one's mind in connection with disappointments and failures of the past, and the broken hearts that occur as the result of the loss of material things or the loss of friends or loved ones.

Self-discipline is the only real solution for such problems. It begins with the recognition of the fact that there are only two kinds of problems: those you can solve, and those you can't solve.

The problem which can be solved should immediately be cleared by the most practical means available, and those which have no solution should be put out of your mind and forgotten.

Let us think, for a minute, about this process of forgetting. Refer to it as closing the door on some unpleasantness which is disturbing your emotional equilibrium. Self-discipline, which means mastery over all emotions, can enable you to close the door between yourself and the unpleasant experience of the past. You must close the door tightly and lock it securely, so that there is no possibility of its being opened again. This is the way to treat unsolvable problems, too. Those who lack self-discipline often stand in the doorway and look wistfully backward into the past, instead of closing the door and looking forward into the future.

This door closing is a valuable technique. It requires the support of a good, strong will, and you have a strong will if you have the departments of your mind organized and under the control of your ego, as they should be.

Door closing does not make you hard, cold or unemotional, but it does require firmness. Self-discipline cannot permit lurking memories of sad experiences, and it wastes no time worrying over problems which have no solution. You cannot yield to the temptation to relive your unhappy memories, for they destroy your creative force, undermine your initiative, weaken your imagination, disturb your faculty of reason, and generally confuse the departments of your mind.

You must place the power of your will against the door that shuts out that which you wish to forget, or you do not acquire self-discipline. This is one of the major services self-discipline can perform for you. It closes the door tightly against all manner of fears, and opens wide the doors of hope and faith!

Self-discipline closes the door against jealousy, hatred, revenge, greed, anger and superstition, and opens the door to friendship, goodwill, confidence and love.

Self-discipline looks forward, not backward. It roots out discouragement and worry and other negative emotions. And it not only encourages the positive emotions, but it forces them to come before the faculty of reason every time they express themselves so that they, too, may be kept under control.

Self-discipline makes your mind strong. It enables you to take possession of your mind and exercise your God-given right to control your mental attitude. You do not have real self-discipline until you organize your mind and keep it clear of all disturbing influences. Every principle of this philosophy must function through your mind, and self-discipline, which keeps your mind orderly, is the controlling factor in this process of becoming successful.

Source: *PMA Science of Success*. Pgs. 286, 287 & 288.

JAICO PUBLISHING HOUSE

Elevate Your Life. Transform Your World.

ESTABLISHED IN 1946, Jaico Publishing House is home to world-transforming authors such as Sri Sri Paramahansa Yogananda, Osho, The Dalai Lama, Sri Sri Ravi Shankar, Robin Sharma, Deepak Chopra, Jack Canfield, Eknath Easwaran, Devdutt Pattanaik, Khushwant Singh, John Maxwell, Brian Tracy and Stephen Hawking.

Our late founder Mr. Jaman Shah first established Jaico as a book distribution company. Sensing that independence was around the corner, he aptly named his company Jaico ('Jai' means victory in Hindi). In order to service the significant demand for affordable books in a developing nation, Mr. Shah initiated Jaico's own publications. Jaico was India's first publisher of paperback books in the English language.

While self-help, religion and philosophy, mind/body/spirit, and business titles form the cornerstone of our non-fiction list, we publish an exciting range of travel, current affairs, biography, and popular science books as well. Our renewed focus on popular fiction is evident in our new titles by a host of fresh young talent from India and abroad. Jaico's recently established Translations Division translates selected English content into nine regional languages.

Jaico's Higher Education Division (HED) is recognized for its student-friendly textbooks in Business Management and Engineering which are in use countrywide.

In addition to being a publisher and distributor of its own titles, Jaico is a major national distributor of books of leading international and Indian publishers. With its headquarters in Mumbai, Jaico has branches and sales offices in Ahmedabad, Bangalore, Bhopal, Bhubaneswar, Chennai, Delhi, Hyderabad, Kolkata and Lucknow.

SINCE 1946